Fuel Cells

The Power Generation Series

Paul Breeze—Coal-Fired Generation, ISBN 13: 9780128040065
Paul Breeze—Gas-Turbine Fired Generation, ISBN 13: 9780128040058
Paul Breeze—Solar Power Generation, ISBN 13: 9780128040041
Paul Breeze—Wind Power Generation, ISBN 13: 9780128040386
Paul Breeze—Fuel Cells, ISBN 13: 9780081010396
Paul Breeze—Energy from Waste, ISBN 13: 9780081010426
Paul Breeze—Nuclear Power, ISBN 13: 9780081010433
Paul Breeze—Electricity Generation and the Environment, ISBN 13: 9780081010440

Fuel Cells

Paul Breeze

ACADEMIC PRESS

An imprint of Elsevier
elsevier.com

Academic Press is an imprint of Elsevier
125 London Wall, London EC2Y 5AS, United Kingdom
525 B Street, Suite 1800, San Diego, CA 92101-4495, United States
50 Hampshire Street, 5th Floor, Cambridge, MA 02139, United States
The Boulevard, Langford Lane, Kidlington, Oxford OX5 1GB, United Kingdom

Notices
Knowledge and best practice in this field are constantly changing. As new research and
experience broaden our understanding, changes in research methods, professional practices,
or medical treatment may become necessary.

Practitioners and researchers must always rely on their own experience and knowledge in
evaluating and using any information, methods, compounds, or experiments described herein.
In using such information or methods they should be mindful of their own safety and the safety
of others, including parties for whom they have a professional responsibility.

To the fullest extent of the law, neither the Publisher nor the authors, contributors, or editors,
assume any liability for any injury and/or damage to persons or property as a matter of products
liability, negligence or otherwise, or from any use or operation of any methods, products,
instructions, or ideas contained in the material herein.

British Library Cataloguing-in-Publication Data
A catalogue record for this book is available from the British Library

Library of Congress Cataloging-in-Publication Data
A catalog record for this book is available from the Library of Congress

ISBN: 978-0-08-101039-6

For Information on all Academic Press publications
visit our website at https://www.elsevier.com/books-and-journals

Working together
to grow libraries in
developing countries

www.elsevier.com • www.bookaid.org

Publisher: Joe Hayton
Acquisition Editor: Maria Convey
Editorial Project Manager: Mariana Kuhl
Production Project Manager: Mohana Natarajan

Typeset by MPS Limited, Chennai, India

CONTENTS

CHAPTER 1

An Introduction to Fuel Cells

The fuel cell is an electrochemical device, similar in concept to a battery, that exploits a chemical reaction in order to generate electricity. Batteries are designed as portable sources of electrical power and so they must carry all the chemicals necessary to provide that power within them. Once those chemicals are exhausted, the battery can no longer provide any power. A fuel cell, in contrast, contains no chemical fuel itself. It simply provides a reaction chamber in which the fuel cell reaction takes place. The actual reactants that are needed to generate the electricity are provided externally. So long as there is a source of the chemical fuel, the fuel cell can generate power. Some fuel cells are still designed to be portable, like batteries. However, many are designed for stationary applications and have very limited portability.

In order for a chemical reaction to be able to provide electrical power, it must be a reaction that releases energy as it proceeds. Such reactions are called exothermic. When a reaction of this type takes place under normal conditions, by mixing the ingredients together in a test tube for example, this energy is released in the form of heat. By manipulation of the reaction conditions, the battery and the fuel cell both release most of that energy as electrical energy instead of heat energy.

There are a wide variety of exothermic chemical reactions that have proved suitable for battery construction, reactions such as that between lead and sulfuric acid that forms the basis of the lead-acid battery used to start motor vehicles. Fuel cells, however, virtually all rely on a single reaction, that between hydrogen and oxygen to produce water. (The one variation involves a reaction between methanol and oxygen that produces carbon dioxide and water.)

The simplicity of the fuel cell reaction and the benign reaction product, water, makes the fuel cell extremely attractive environmentally. In addition, the fact that the driving force is electrochemical rather than thermodynamic means that fuel cells are not limited by heat-engine

Fuel Cells. DOI: http://dx.doi.org/10.1016/B978-0-08-101039-6.00001-7

physics and are potentially more efficient than most alternative fuel-based forms of power generation. So while the best efficiency for a simple heat engine is that achieved by the diesel engine at around 50% fuel-to-electricity efficiency, the best fuel cell can reach 60%. In fact the theoretical maximum efficiency for a fuel cell operating at room temperature is 83%.

While the fuel cell reaction is simple, the practical realization of a fuel cell is not so straight-forward. In the first place the reaction between hydrogen and oxygen will not take place spontaneously at ambient temperature,[1] so the reaction must be catalyzed in low temperature fuel cells. In addition, while the oxygen that is required by a fuel cell can be provided from air, there is no ready source of hydrogen today. This means that the hydrogen for a fuel cell must be manufactured and in most fuel cells this is achieved by carrying out a process called reforming with natural gas. Reforming natural gas produces hydrogen but also generates carbon dioxide so that one of the clear environmental benefits of the fuel cell reaction, that it produces only water, is no longer applicable. In addition, the reforming of natural gas has an energy penalty, so that a fuel cell using natural gas is not as efficient as one that is fueled with pure hydrogen.

In the future there may be ready sources of hydrogen available. In the meantime, fuel cells remain environmentally attractive because of other advantages they possess. The device itself has no moving parts making it inherently quiet and relatively maintenance free. (Some fuel cell systems require pumps which will generate noise.) And even when fueled with natural gas the fuel cell generates little in the way of atmospheric or other pollutants excepting carbon dioxide. This makes it easy to site fuel cell power plants in urban areas where systems based on rotating machines such as gas turbines, steam turbines, or reciprocating engines are often less suitable.

While fuel cells offer some major advantages over other power generation technologies, one factor has held them back commercially, their cost. The principle of the fuel cell has been known since the first half of the 19th century but it was not until the middle of the 20th century that a practical fuel cell was built. The first cells were very efficient alkaline fuel cells. These demonstrated the potential for fuel cell

---

[1]The reaction can be started with a spark or flame, resulting in an uncontrolled chain reaction.

technology but also highlighted its weakness. In order to make a fuel cell work, it was necessary to provide a catalyst that was formed from a very expensive material such as platinum. Partly as a result of this, the first fuel cells proved prohibitively expensive to make and operate.

Early fuel cells were adopted by NASA for its manned space program, an application where cost was immaterial provided the device could function efficiently and reliably. Meanwhile research during the second half of the 20th century led to the development of a range of new fuel cell technologies. Eventually a commercial fuel cell for stationary power applications was launched in 1992 based on one of these new technologies, the phosphoric acid fuel cell. Costs were still high but continued development has brought the costs of this technology down. In addition, the automotive industry has identified another type of fuel cell, the proton exchange membrane fuel, cell as a potential automotive power source to replace the piston engine and this has led to heavy investment into this area of fuel cell research. Meanwhile other technologies including two high-temperature fuel cells, the solid oxide fuel cell, and the molten carbonate fuel cell are being developed for stationary power applications and the direct methanol fuel cell has potential for portable power use.

In spite of continued investment, fuel cells have not yet had a major impact on global power generation. The global installed capacity of stationary fuel cells was over 1000 MW, but probably well under 2000 MW, at the end of 2015 based on shipment data.[2] This may be compared to a global installed power generating capacity from all technologies of around 6,200,000 MW at the end of 2014[3]: fuel cells provide 0.02% of this. It may require the development of a clean energy economy built around hydrogen rather than fossil fuels to boost growth rates significantly. Such an economy would allow fuel cells to achieve their full potential. The development of this economy is likely to be tied to the growth in the use of fuel cells in automotive applications.

1.1 THE HISTORY OF FUEL CELLS

The history of the fuel cell can be traced to experimental studies of the origins of electricity and its connection to chemical reactions, studies

[2]The shipment data comes from Fuel Cell Energy and E4tech.
[3]World Energy Outlook 2015, International Energy Agency.

that were taking place at the end of the 18th and the beginning of the 19th centuries. One of the scientists involved in this endeavor was the British scientist Sir Humphry Davy. Davy studied the effect of an electric current on water and showed that the passage of a current could split water into hydrogen and oxygen, the process now known as the electrolysis of water. In 1802 he also devised a very simple electrochemical cell using oxygen that was able to deliver a small electric shock. This device had a carbon anode and nitric acid electrolyte but Davy did not publish his findings.

While Davy's device is now recognized as a crude form of fuel cell, the first fuel cell that conforms to the modern description was a device that was developed independently by the German scientist Christian Friedrich Schonbein and the British scientist William Grove. Both men were exploring the idea that if water could be split into its constituent elements by an electrical current, then the process could be reversed and hydrogen and oxygen used to generate a current. Grove's letter on the subject was published in *The London and Edinburgh Philosophical Magazine and Journal of Science* in December 1838, Schonbein's in 1839 and in consequence Grove is now considered the father of the fuel cell.

Grove's fuel cell consisted of an electrolytic solution of sulfuric acid into which electrodes were placed. Hydrogen was delivered to one electrode, oxygen to the other in a cell that is similar in concept to the modern phosphoric acid fuel cell. Grove called the devices gas voltaic batteries although they were also called Grove cells. The actual name "fuel cell" was first used in 1889 by Charles Langer and Ludwig Mond who were trying to develop a practical cell from Grove's work using coal gas and oxygen. The cell never achieved practical success and research was largely abandoned in the 1900s after the development of the internal combustion engine.

The next milestone in fuel cell development came in 1930s when another British scientist, Francis Bacon, began to study the alkaline fuel cell. Bacon pursued his interest initially as an amateur inventor but later was able to organize research teams to develop the fuel cell. This culminated, in 1959, with the demonstration of a 5 kW "Bacon Cell." In the same year, engineer Henry Ihrig, working for the Allis Chalmers Manufacturing Company, built a 15 kW fuel cell stack of 1008 cells based on the alkaline fuel cell and used it to power a tractor. The company later built a golf cart, a submersible and a fork lift truck powered by fuel cells.

Bacon patented the design he had developed and in the early 1960s the Pratt and Whitney Aircraft Corporation licensed the Bacon Cell and began to develop the technology. The company was able to develop an alkaline fuel cell that attracted the attention of NASA and was subsequently used in the Apollo space program. The company's fuel cells were able to supply both power and drinking water to the astronauts on manned space flights and were later used on the space shuttle too. Pratt and Whitney was eventually taken over by United Technologies Corporation (UTC).

In 1955, at the same time as Bacon was developing his fuel cell, Thomas Grubb and Leonard Niedrach, two scientists working for general electric (GE) developed a different type of fuel cell that used a proton exchange membrane as its electrolyte. This too attracted the interest of NASA which was looking for a power source for its Gemini space program, the forerunner of Apollo. The GE proton exchange membrane fuel cell was eventually adopted for later Gemini flights before being replaced by the alkaline fuel cell for Apollo. The cell was also developed for marine use and was adopted in the 1980s by the UK Royal Navy for its submarine fleet. The proton exchange membrane fuel cell, which is extremely light, has since subsequently attracted the attention of vehicle manufacturers. It is now the main type of fuel cell being developed for automotive power.

The oil crises of the 1970s spurred research into a range of alternative technologies for power generation that included fuel cells as well as most of the new renewable technologies in use today. The fuel cell research from that period laid the foundations for the development of several new types of fuel cell including the phosphoric acid fuel cell, the solid oxide fuel cell, and the molten carbonate fuel cell. The last two are high-temperature fuel cells that operate under conditions that allow hydrogen and oxygen to react much more easily than at room temperature. To this list of fuel cell types was added the direct methanol fuel cell in the 1990s, a device that is particularly suited to mobile and portable applications. More recent additions include the proposal to use a perovskite crystal as the electrolyte in a fuel cell and the development of microbial fuel cells.

While development of fuel cell technology expanded during the 1980s, the commercialization of the technology was held back by cost. The fuel cells being used by NASA were too expensive for general use so cheaper alternatives were required if the technology was ever to find a market. It was not until the 1990s that the first commercial station- ary fuel cell was launched, a phosphoric acid fuel cell system developed by International Fuel Cells, a subsidiary of UTC and Toshiba.[4] There were also developments in Japan at around the same time based on the same fuel cell technology. However, fuel cells remained relatively expensive and it was not until the following decade that the costs fell sufficiently for a commercial market to begin to develop. Since then the market has expanded, slowly, for all the main types of fuel cell.

1.2 GLOBAL FUEL CELL CAPACITY

In spite of the interest in fuel cells, creating a market for the devices has been difficult. Volumes are picking up slowly but the technologies have a long way to go before they can compete with other mainstream power generation technologies in terms of installed capacity. Fuel cells that are being manufactured today address three main markets, power units for portable devices, stationary power generation applications, and transportation applications. For portable devices the direct methanol fuel cell and the proton exchange membrane fuel cells appear to be the most popular while the most successful for transportation is the proton exchange membrane fuel cell. All can potentially be used for stationary power generation applications but the choice may depend on the size of the generation unit required. Meanwhile, one of the high-temperature fuel cells, the solid oxide fuel cell is finding a market as a domestic heat and power unit alongside proton exchange membrane fuel cell units.

Table 1.1 shows figures for the annual shipments of fuel cells between 2007 and 2015. These figures offer the best approximation to the actual capacity being installed each year. In the first year in the table, 2007, an estimated 37.1 MW of cells were shipped by manufac- turers across the globe. The total capacity shipped rose to 51.1 MW in 2008 and 86.5 MW in 2009, in 2011 the 100 MW barrier was passed for the first time with shipment of 109.4 MW and in 2013 the 200 MW barrier was exceeded when 215.3 MW of fuel cells were shipped. The overall capacity fell back in 2014 to 185.4 MW but rose significantly in 2015 to 342.6 MW.

---

[4]This technology is now owned an marketed by Korean company Doosan.

Table 1.1 Annual Shipments of Fuel Cells[5]

Year	Annual Shipment of Fuel Cells (MW)
2007	37.1
2008	51.1
2009	86.5
2010	91.2
2011	109.4
2012	166.7
2013	215.3
2014	185.4
2015	342.6
Source: Fuel Cells Today, E4tech.	

Table 1.2 Fuel Cell Shipments by Region, 2015[6]

Region	Fuel Cell Shipments in 2015 (MW)
Europe	28.5
North America	139.7
Asia	172.2
Rest of the world	2.2
Total	342.6
Source: E4tech.	

The actual number of fuel cell units shipped in 2015 was 71,500. This is only slightly higher than in 2014 when 63,600 units were shipped. The discrepancy is explained by the fact that fewer small units were shipped in 2015 than in 2014.

The markets for fuel cells remain limited and the biggest markets, particularly for stationary power generation applications are in countries where there is government support for fuel cell development. In 2015 the largest regional market was Asia. A total of 172.2 MW of the total shipments in 2015 went to this region, as shown in Table 1.2. The main markets in this region are Japan where the use of domestic

[5]The Fuel Cell Today Industry Review 2011–13 published by Fuel Cell Today, Fuel Cell Industry Review 2015 published by E4tech.
[6]Fuel Cell Industry Review 2015, E4tech.

combined heat and power units is being promoted and South Korea where a number of stationary fuel cell power plants were installed. The introduction of fuel cell cars in Japan has also boosted sales there. The second largest region in terms of shipments in 2015 was North America. Here the main market sector appears to be stationary fuel cells for power generation in the United States. There are also signs of increased vehicle sales in North America. European fuel cell shipments were small compared to both these regions, with 28.5 MW shipped in 2015. The European market sectors include both domestic and commercial scale combined heat and power, large scale stationary power, and fuel cell backup systems. Installations in the rest of the world are limited with only 2.2 MW in total in 2015.

The shipments of fuel cells in 2015 are broken down by type in Table 1.3. These figures show that the most popular fuel cell type, in terms of megawatts shipped was the proton exchange membrane fuel cell. This accounted for 179.6 MW of the total that year. This was also true in terms of the number of units shipped, with 63,800 of this type of cell sent out in 2015, 89% of the total number that year. Many of these units were destined either for transportation applications or domestic combined heat and power. At the other end of the scale, the smallest shipment volumes in terms of megawatts were for the direct methanol fuel cell and the alkaline fuel cell. The alkaline fuel cell is still finding its market so very few units of the cell were shipped. The number of direct methanol fuel cells shipped was 2200, most of them very small.

The three other types of fuel cell in Table 1.3 are primarily used for stationary power generation. Of the three the most popular was the

Table 1.3 Fuel Cell Shipments by Type, 2015[6]	
Fuel Cell Type	Fuel Cell Shipments in 2015 (MW)
Proton exchange membrane fuel cell	179.6
Direct methanol fuel cell	0.2
Phosphoric acid fuel cell	24.0
Solid oxide fuel cell	63.1
Molten carbonate fuel cell	75.6
Alkaline fuel cell	0.2
Total	242.6
Source: E4tech.	

molten carbonate fuel cell which shipped 75.6 MW in 2015, and 100 units. The phosphoric acid fuel cell shipped 24.0 MW, again with 100 units. Meanwhile the solid oxide fuel cell shipped 63.1 MW in 5400 units. The large number of solid oxide fuel cell units reflect its use in small domestic power supplies.

Table 1.4 presents figures for the shipments in 2015 broken down by market sectors. In this case the largest market sector is that for stationary power generation which accounted for 203.2 MW of the total that year. Transportation applications accounted for most of the remainder with 138.7 MW while portable applications only accounted for 700 kW. In terms of the numbers of fuel cell units shipped, there were 49,000 for stationary power generation applications, 4900 units for transportation, and 17,600 units destined for portable applications.

The primary area of interest in this book is the use of fuel cells for stationary power applications. As already noted, some of the

Table 1.4 Fuel Cell Shipments by Application, 2015[6]	
Application	Fuel Cell Shipments in 2015 (MW)
Portable applications	0.7
Stationary applications	203.2
Transportation applications	138.7
Source: E4tech.	

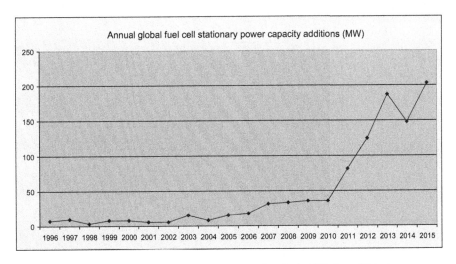

Figure 1.1 Annual stationary fuel cell installations. Source: Data from Fuel Cell Today and E4tech.

technologies are better suited to this type of applications while others have a wider range of uses. The technology chapters later in the book will indicate the most important applications for each type of fuel cell. However, all the main technologies are potentially useful for stationary power generation.

Fig. 1.1 shows the annual installation, by generating capacity, of stationary fuel cells between 1996 and 2015.[7] During the 1990s the level of annual installations was generally under 10 MW. The volumes of installations began to rise slowly from around 2003 and by the end of the first decade of the 21st century they were around 30 MW each year. Since then the annual installation rate has begun to rise much more steeply, with the exception of a fall in 2014, reaching 203 MW in 2015.

[7]2008 Large Stationary Survey, Kerry-Ann Adamson, Fuel Cell Today 2008, Fuel Cell Industry Review, Fuel Cell Today and E4tech, 2009–2015.

CHAPTER 2

The Fundamentals of Fuel Cell Operation

The fuel cell is an electrochemical device similar to a battery that converts energy released during a chemical reaction into electricity. In order to achieve this the cell has to control carefully the way in which the chemical reactants that are introduced into the cell interact with one another so that electrical power can be extracted.

A typical fuel cell consists of a thin layer of an electrolyte material sandwiched between two electrodes so that the latter are in intimate contact with the electrolyte. There will be external systems to deliver the fuel, normally oxygen and hydrogen, to the two electrodes. The gases must be able to spread easily through the electrode structures, which are porous, in order to react at the electrode–electrolyte interface. Meanwhile electrical contacts at the electrodes allow the fuel cell to be connected to an external circuit.

The electrolyte in the fuel cell is essentially a semi-permeable membrane that will allow a charged atom or molecule, such as a hydrogen ion, H^+, to pass from one electrode to the other—it will conduct hydrogen ions—but that will not conduct electrons. However, the exchange of electrons between the chemical species which form at the electrodes is essential for the reaction to take place. Therefore the chemical reaction within the fuel cell can only take place when an electrical circuit is made so that electrons flowing from one electrode to the other through this external circuit can complete the reaction.

Since the reactants in the fuel cell are gases, the electrodes of the cell must be designed to provide an interface where the gas molecules can react as well as allowing charged molecular species formed during the fuel cell reaction to pass either into or out of the electrolyte, which may be a liquid or a solid. Depending on the design and the temperature at which the cell operates, this will require the use of a catalyst to promote the molecular processes that must take place at the gas/liquid or gas/solid interface.

Fuel Cells. DOI: http://dx.doi.org/10.1016/B978-0-08-101039-6.00002-9

Most fuel cells require hydrogen to operate. Since this is not readily available, fuel cells instead burn natural gas which is converted into hydrogen is a device called a reformer. This reformer is an integral part of the fuel cell. In addition, many fuel cells also generate significant amounts of heat. The most efficient fuel cell systems will reuse this heat either to generate more electricity or to provide heat energy in a combined heat and power system.

2.1 THE FUEL CELL PRINCIPLE

The principle upon which the fuel cell operates belongs to a branch of chemistry called electro-chemistry. This explores how electricity can be derived from a chemical reaction. In nature certain materials will react with one another spontaneously if the conditions are correct. For example, a strong acid such as sulfuric acid will react vigorously with a variety of different metals if they are mixed with it. All that is necessary is to place a piece of the metal into the acid. Other reactions will proceed spontaneously but require a kick start. Typical of these is the reaction between hydrogen with oxygen. The two gases can be mixed at ambient temperatures without any reaction but once the temperature is raised beyond a certain point, with a spark for example, the reaction will proceed explosively.

Spontaneous reactions occur in nature because the products of the reaction are more stable than the starting materials. Reactions of this type are called exothermic reactions because they all release heat energy when they are allowed to proceed freely. This heat energy is equivalent to the difference in stability between reactants and products. In order to reverse the reaction, this amount of energy—or more—would have to be provided to the reaction products to push the reaction backwards.

All the chemical reactions that can be used to generate electrical energy in batteries and fuel cells are spontaneous reactions. When such a reaction is exploited electrochemically, the progress of the reaction is managed in such a way that some of the energy that would normally be released as heat emerges instead as electrical energy.

The reaction between hydrogen and oxygen is exothermic. This reaction can be expressed by a simple chemical formula:

$$2H_2 + O_2 = 2H_2O$$

The formula shows two hydrogen molecules and one oxygen molecule reacting to create two molecules of water. Although the formula looks simple, this is in fact a relatively complex process but it can be broken down into three simple partial reactions, each of which must take place for the reaction to run to completion. The first of these involves the hydrogen molecule, H_2, splitting into two hydrogen atoms, H, and the each of these releasing an electron to form a positively charged hydrogen ion, a proton:

$$H_2 = 2H^+ + 2e^-$$

A parallel second partial reaction involves the oxygen molecule, O_2, which splits into two oxygen atoms, O. Each of these absorbs two electrons released from two hydrogen atoms to produce a doubly negatively charged oxygen ion, O^{2-}:

$$O_2 + 4e^- = 2O^{2-}$$

The third and final part of the reaction involves the negatively charged oxygen ion attracting two positively charged hydrogen atoms and the three ions coalescing to form a water molecule, H_2O:

$$O^{2-} + 2H^+ = H_2O$$

Then the reaction is complete.

This reaction will not take place spontaneously at ambient temperatures because a significant amount of energy is required to rupture the bonds holding the oxygen atoms together in the oxygen molecule and the hydrogen atoms together in the hydrogen molecule. At high temperatures, these molecules will begin to dissociate spontaneously. Once dissociation begins and free oxygen and hydrogen atoms are available, these will react together very rapidly, releasing in the process much more energy that was needed to rupture the molecular H_2 and O_2 bonds. The high temperature in a spark is sufficient to initiate the reaction. However in a low-temperature fuel cell, the rupture of these bonds and the dissociation of the molecular hydrogen and oxygen must be assisted. This assistance is provided by a catalyst.

When hydrogen burns in air (oxygen), the various steps of the reaction occur in the same place at the same time, not in the stepwise fashion shown above. However in a fuel cell, the hydrogen and oxygen are not allowed to mix. Instead the reacting gases are introduced

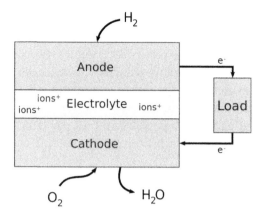

Figure 2.1 The fuel cell principle. Source: Wikipedia.

separately, hydrogen to one electrode of the cell and oxygen to the other. The two electrodes are separated by the electrolyte, as shown in Fig. 2.1.

The electrolyte is the key element in any electrochemical cell because it acts like a filter to both stop the cell reactants mixing directly with one another and to control how the charged ions created during the partial cell reactions are allowed to react with one another. The electrolyte in a fuel cell is impermeable to the gases, hydrogen, and oxygen. It will not conduct electricity in the form of electrons either, nor (provided it is an acidic electrolyte) will it conduct the negatively charged oxygen ions or the more common form in water, the hydroxyl ion (OH^-). What it will do is conduct positively charged hydrogen ions.

So, at the hydrogen electrode (which is called the anode) the hydrogen molecules first adhere to the electrode material as molecules and then separate into atoms, each subsequently releasing an electron to form a positively charged ion as shown in the equation above. In this ionic form the hydrogen can cross the electrolyte boundary and reach the oxygen at the second electrode. The electrons, however, are left behind at the anode.

At the second electrode (called the cathode), oxygen atoms will also adhere to the electrode surface as molecules, then dissociate, each leaving two oxygen atoms. However, these require a supply of electrons if they are to form oxygen ions. Only in this form can they coalesce with the hydrogen ions traveling through the electrolyte from the anode to create water molecules. The electrons must come from the anode, but these electrons cannot pass through the electrolyte.

If an electrical connection is made between the two electrodes, the electrons will pass through the connecting wire to the oxygen atoms where they will create oxygen ions, allowing the reaction to run to completion. When a small electric light bulb is inserted into this circuit, it will glow, proving that an electric current is indeed flowing between one electrode and the other.

All electrochemical cells operate in this way. While part of the reaction can take place within the confines of the cell, it can only be completed if electrons are allowed to travel from one electrode to the other through an external circuit.[1] If no connection is made the exothermic nature of the reaction means that a charge builds up at each electrode, creating an electrical potential, the cell voltage, which will drive electrons from one electrode to the other when a connection is made.

Since the electrolyte is such an important part of an electrochemical cell, fuel cells are generally identified by the type of electrolyte they employ. Phosphoric acid fuel cells (PAFCs) use phosphoric acid, which being acidic is a proton (positively charged hydrogen atom) conductor. Proton exchange membrane cells also rely on an acidic membrane to allow hydrogen ions to pass. The alkaline fuel cell (AFC) is a hydroxide ion (OH^-) conductor; the hydroxide ion is the complement in water of the hydrogen ion. Meanwhile the high temperature solid oxide fuel cell (SOFC) uses a solid that is a conductor of oxygen ions. Other fuel cell reactions appear more complex even though the end result is the same. So, for example, the molten carbonate fuel cell (MCFC) electrolyte conducts carbonate ions.

2.2 CATALYSTS

The description of the operation of a fuel cell above is a simplification, because it omits one key feature of the reaction between hydrogen and oxygen. Although hydrogen atoms and oxygen atoms will react spontaneously to form water, both hydrogen and oxygen are found—at

---

[1]In fact a few electrons can pass through the electrolyte but the latter's electrical resistance to this is very high so little leakage normally takes place.

room temperature—in the molecular forms H_2 and O_2. These hydrogen and oxygen molecules must split into atoms before the reaction will proceed but they will not do so spontaneously because of the chemical bond holding each molecule together, even though these bonds are much weaker than the chemical bonds that will bind them together into a water molecule. The energy needed to cause the individual molecules to dissociated into atoms creates an energy barrier called the activation energy that must be overcome before the highly exothermic reaction between the atoms can take place.

One method of splitting the molecules is to raise their temperature. They will start dissociate spontaneously at between 800°C and 1000°C. A flame or a spark will be hot enough to split sufficient of the molecules to start the reaction which then generates so much heat spontaneously that it keeps the reaction going until all the hydrogen or oxygen is used up. Some fuel cell designs also use high temperatures to encourage the gas molecules to dissociate but high temperatures bring their own design and materials problems.

The alternative is to use a catalyst. A catalyst is a component that is needed for a reaction to take place but that is not actually consumed during the reaction. It is usually used to accelerate a reaction that will otherwise take place very slowly or not at all. In the case of the fuel cell the best catalyst for low temperature acceleration of the reaction is the metal platinum. The platinum acts as a catalyst because both hydrogen and oxygen are attracted to the metal surface where they prefer to stick to it in dissociated form, as atoms, rather than as hydrogen or oxygen molecules. The metal can therefore provide the supply of atoms needed for the fuel cell reaction to take place. In its presence, the reaction can take place at below 100°C.

Platinum, even though it is only required in small quantities in a fuel cell, is expensive and this helps to elevate the cost of the cells themselves. A key area of fuel cell research is therefore directed at finding cheaper alternatives. Platinum is also very sensitive to impurities in the gaseous reactants which can poison it, rendering it ineffective. Sulfur dioxide is a particular problem and so is carbon monoxide, both of which can find their way into hydrogen generated by the reforming of natural gas or other fuels. This is another reason why alternative catalysts, which are less sensitive to poisoning, are being sought.

One area of research focusses on the exploitation of oxygen by natural species including animals and plants. It may not be immediately obvious but in fact both animals and plants exploit the same reaction as the fuel cell, using oxygen as a source of energy. However, animal and plant cells do not require platinum. Instead they use complex organic enzymes that contain metals such as iron and manganese. It may be possible in the future to use similar molecules to catalyze the reaction in fuel cells.

2.3 HYDROCARBON GAS REFORMATION

A fuel cell is designed to "burn" hydrogen and oxygen in order to generate electricity. Hydrogen is not generally available but hydrocarbon gases such as natural gas or even gases generated from biomass can be converted into hydrogen in a process known as reformation. The reformation reaction generates a gas which contains a mixture of carbon dioxide and hydrogen which can then be supplied as a reactant for the fuel cell. (The carbon dioxide will be inert and so will not interfere with reaction other than by acting as a diluent for the hydrogen.) The primary energy-providing constituent of natural gas and of most biogas is methane and this is the main target for the standard reformation process although other hydrocarbons can also be reformed and even coal can be converted into a hydrogen-rich fuel if necessary.

The conversion is usually carried out as a two stage process. In the first stage the methane-rich gas is mixed with water vapor and passed over a catalyst at high temperature where the gases react to produce a mixture of hydrogen and carbon monoxide, a process called steam reforming. A second reaction, called the water shift reaction, is then carried out during which additional water vapor is added to the new mixture where it reacts with the carbon monoxide, again in the presence of a catalyst, to produce more hydrogen and carbon dioxide.

The degree to which this second stage reaction is carried to completion is extremely important for fuel cells because the platinum catalyst in low temperature cells is sensitive to carbon monoxide poisoning. In consequence, virtually all the carbon monoxide must be removed from the fuel before is fed into the fuel cell. Natural gas can also contain some sulfur impurity, an even more vigorous poison. This is normally removed by cleaning the fuel before it is reformed but if not then any remaining sulfur must be removed since low-temperature fuel cell catalysts are extremely sensitive to its presence.

While natural gas is the most convenient source of hydrogen for a fuel cell today, other fuels can also be exploited. For example, methanol can also be converted into a hydrogen-rich gas using a reforming process, as can gasoline, though the latter requires an extremely high temperature (800°C). Both these processes are of interest to the automotive industry. There is also a low-temperature fuel cell that can reform methanol directly at the cell electrode but this cell is relatively inefficient compared to cells that use hydrogen directly.

Since reforming of these fuels normally takes place at a relatively high-temperature, low-temperature fuel cells have to be equipped with an external reformer to process the fuel before it enters the fuel cell. The conditions inside the two main types of high-temperature fuel cell are sufficient for the reforming to take place within the cell itself, simplifying system design.

While a fuel cell burning hydrogen and oxygen produces no carbon dioxide, most fuel cells will generate carbon dioxide because they derive their hydrogen from natural gas or another carbon containing fuel. When methane is converted into hydrogen, it generates exactly the same amount of carbon monoxide as it would have generated if it had been burned in a gas turbine. However, if hydrogen can be generated without the need for fossil fuel combustion, by using renewable energy to electrolyze water, for example, then burning the gas in a fuel cell provides an efficient and emission free source of electricity.

2.4 FUEL CELL EFFICIENCY

The reaction between hydrogen and oxygen to create water releases a precisely quantified amount of energy. Not all this energy can be converted into electricity because some is required to overcome the energy barrier that normally prevents the reaction proceeding. When this reaction takes place between oxygen and hydrogen, each provided at a pressure of one atmosphere and at room temperature, the theoretical maximum chemical-to-electrical energy conversion efficiency that can be achieved is 83%. This efficiency is a theoretical ideal and no cell would be able to achieve that figure.

The precise reaction conditions affect the potential efficiency too. If the pressure of the reacting gases is increased, then conversion efficiency can be increased. On the other hand, increasing the operating temperature of the cell will reduce the overall efficiency that can be achieved.

The actual conversion efficiency of a fuel cell is reflected in the voltage that the cell produces between its terminals. The theoretical maximum cell voltage at open circuit for a fuel cell operating at room temperature, when the cell is delivering no current, is 1.229 V. In practice such a cell would deliver a voltage less than this because of losses resulting from the internal resistance of the cell and activation energy barriers of various sorts at electrode interfaces.

This theoretical maximum voltage only applies to a cell where the cell reaction product is water in liquid form. In most practical cells, where because of the operating temperature the product is actually water vapor, this maximum falls further. At 100°C the ideal cell voltage is 1.16 V and at 800°C the ideal cell voltage is only 0.99 V. This is equivalent to a maximum ideal efficiency of 67%. In practice, high temperature cells can achieve 50%–60% efficiency. Low cells have the potential to reach higher efficiency still but in practice the best that has been achieved is 60% efficiency.

While high temperature cells are ostensibly less efficient, the loss of electrochemical efficiency is not necessarily a major handicap. The heat generated within the cells can be exploited either to produce more electricity in some form of hybrid system or it may be utilized in a combined heat and power system, providing useful heat as well as electricity.

2.5 FUEL CELL TYPES

There are six types of fuel cell that are commercially available today. These six are the AFC, the proton exchange membrane fuel cell (PEMFC, sometimes also called a polymer electrolyte membrane fuel cell), the PAFC, the MCFC, the SOFC, and the direct methanol fuel cell (DMFC). These cells are often identified simply by their acronyms. Some of the characteristics of these fuel cells are shown in Table 2.1.

Table 2.1 Characteristics of Main Fuel Cell Types			
Fuel Cell	Typical Operating Temperature (°C)	Typical Size	Efficiency
AFC	<100	1−100 kW	>60%
PEMFC	<120	1−100 kW	60% with hydrogen 40% with reformed fuel
PAFC	150−200	5−400 kW	40%
MCFC	600−700	300−3000 kW	50%
SOFC	500−1000	1−1000 kW	60%
DMFC	60−130	1 W−100 kW	40%
Source: US Department of Energy, Fuel Cell Today.			

The AFC is one of the most efficient fuel cells and operates at a relatively low temperature for a fuel cell. It was the first type of fuel cell to be fully developed and was used in the US space program. However, it has traditionally been considered expensive compared to other types. Recent advances are making it more competitive.

The PEMFC was also developed early in the modern history of fuel cells and it too was used in the US space program by NASA. The cell operates at a relatively low temperature and is very efficient when provided with pure hydrogen, less efficient when using reformed natural gas. The cell has received considerable attention and investment as a potential power source for vehicles due to its low weight.

The PAFC was the first fuel cell to be made available commercially, in the early 1990s. The technology was relatively expensive at that time and was expected to be superseded by cheaper alternatives but it made a strong comeback in the first decade of the 21st century and continues to compete with the other main types.

The MCFC is a high-temperature fuel cell that is able to reform natural gas internally. The fuel cell is more complex that the other main types and is only economically effective in larger sizes. However, it has been one of the most successful fuel cells for large stationary applications.

The SOFC is another high-temperature fuel cell. It is unique in having a solid state electrolyte with makes the cell potentially very robust. The fuel cell is suitable for both small and large installations.

The DMFC is the most recent addition to the stable of commercial fuel cells. Unlike the other fuel cells, it will "burn" methanol rather than hydrogen and this has made it attractive both for very small fuel cells for portable devices such as mobile phones and computers and as a potential power source for vehicles.

There are other types of fuel cell being developed but none has yet reached the stage where it is capable of being offered commercially. One of the most important branches is the development of microbial fuel cells that can exploit the reactions of microbes to produce electricity. Microbes use a variety of organic materials as fuel in order to generate energy. By diverting the normal reaction pathway in the same way as a conventional fuel cell diverts the natural way in which hydrogen and oxygen react, a microbial fuel cell can potentially use natural processes to produce electricity. These types of cell generally provide low power levels which is likely to limit their application to low power micro-electronic devices. Their advantage is that they can produce power from natural sources and so would not need providing with a source of hydrogen and oxygen.

Another area of interest involves the search for alternative solid state materials that can be used as electrolytes in fuel cells. Finding solids that will conduct ions but not electrons is the key and so far the range of materials has been limited. However, a class of crystalline materials called perovskites has recently been considered promising. There is still a long way to go before they might be used in commercial fuel cells but interest and investment is growing.

CHAPTER *3*

The Alkaline Fuel Cell

The alkaline fuel cell (AFC) employs an electrolyte composed of a concentrated alkaline solution. The normal alkali used is potassium hydroxide which is the alkali with the highest conductivity of the alkaline hydroxides. The alkaline solution encourages the oxygen reaction at the cathode of the AFC to occur more quickly than in an acidic electrolyte and this leads to a higher efficiency for similar cell conditions. The earliest cell of this type, developed by British scientist Francis Bacon, used potassium hydroxide at a concentration of 45%.

This high cathode efficiency also allows AFCs to operate with non-precious metal catalysts such as nickel. However, these metals tend to oxidize easily at the oxygen electrode, which can reduce efficiency, so in practice most low-temperature AFCs have used the same platinum catalysts as other types of low-temperature fuel cell. Higher temperature cells can function effectively with a nickel oxide cathode and Bacon's cell, which operated at over 200°C, was constructed using simple nickel electrodes.

The first practical cells of this type, which were used by NASA, also operated at high temperature with nickel electrodes. Here, and elsewhere, the cells have achieved practical efficiencies of greater that 60% and the AFC may be capable of 70% efficiency.

In spite of this high efficiency, the development of AFCs has been hampered by the reactivity of the alkaline electrolyte with carbon dioxide from air, leading to the formation of carbonates which can poison the cell. Cells used in the space were fueled with pure oxygen but the high level of purity needed makes terrestrial use of pure oxygen expensive. Most terrestrial cells have attempted to use air that has been purged of carbon dioxide. This generally leaves some carbon dioxide contamination and so must be combined with a way of cleaning the electrolyte to remove any carbonate formed. Strategies of this type may offer a more cost effective solution for less safety-critical

Fuel Cells. DOI: http://dx.doi.org/10.1016/B978-0-08-101039-6.00003-0

applications. However, the perceived problems with AFCs has led to reduced investment in the technology compared to some other fuel cell types.

3.1 THE HISTORY OF AFCs

The originator of the AFC was the British scientist Francis Bacon who decided to use an alkaline instead of an acidic electrolyte when he began experimenting with fuel cells in the 1930s. Previous cells had all used acid electrolytes. In addition to the new type of electrolyte, Bacon also introduced gas diffusion electrodes in order to increase the surface area at the gas–electrode–electrolyte interface. This type of electrode is now standard in many fuel cells. The electrodes were made of nickel.

Bacon continued to work on the development of his cell from the 1930s until the end of the 1950s when he was able to unveil a practical "Bacon cell." This was a heavy, high-pressure device that operated at around 40 atmospheres. Bacon also chose a relatively high operating temperature of 205°C. Under these conditions, there was no need for a precious metal catalyst to be coated onto the nickel electrodes. The high pressure ensured that the alkali did not boil at the high operating temperature and the gas feeds were pressurized to a slightly higher pressure to ensure that the tiny pores in the electrodes were kept open and did not flood. Bacon's work culminated in the demonstration of a 5 kW fuel cell stack which he unveiled in 1959.

By the 1950s the technology had also been picked up by a number of companies including the Allis Chalmers Manufacturing Company. One of this company's engineers, Henry Ihrig, built a 15 kW fuel cell stack of 1008 cells based on the AFC and used it to power a tractor. The company continued research into the technology and later built a golf cart, a submersible and a fork-lift truck powered by fuel cells. Another company, Union Carbide, also investigated the technology and developed carbon gas diffusion electrodes. Their work led to the development of both a fuel cell powered radio and a fuel cell motorbike for the US Army.

It was a third company, the aircraft engine manufacturer Pratt and Whitney, that made the major breakthrough for AFCs. The company licensed patents from Bacon and used his work as the basis for a fuel cell that it proposed to NASA for the US manned space program. The bid was successful and the work culminated in a 1.5 kW power plant that was used to power the Apollo space missions. The space power unit needed to be light so pressure was reduced to just over 3 atmospheres, enabling a more lightly built cell to be used. In order to prevent the electrolyte boiling at this lower pressure, the concentration of potassium hydroxide was raised from 45% to 75% and the temperature then had to be raised to 260°C to ensure the electrolyte remained liquid. However, nickel electrodes were maintained. The device was able to provide a peak power of 2295 W and ran for 690 h without failing.

The design was subsequently modified for the space shuttle and a lower operating temperature chosen. This required platinum to catalyze the reaction but provided a reliable power unit that was used throughout the space orbiter program.

3.2 THE AFC PRINCIPLE

The cell reaction in the AFC is slightly different to the standard fuel cell reaction because the electrolyte conducts hydroxyl ions (OH^-) rather than protons (H^+) so it is these that mediate the cell reaction. Molecular hydrogen is supplied to the anode where it splits into hydrogen atoms which each release an electron to the external circuit of the cell. These positively charged hydrogen ions then react with hydroxyl ions from the electrolyte to form water molecules at the anode. Meanwhile at the cathode, oxygen molecules dissociate to form oxygen atoms which take electrons from the external circuit and then react with water molecules in the electrolyte to create hydroxyl ions. The reactions at each electrode are shown below:

$$\text{Anode reaction: } 2H_2 + 4OH^- = 4H_2O + 4e^-$$

$$\text{Cathode reaction: } O_2 + 2H_2O + 4e^- = 4OH^-$$

$$\text{Overall reaction: } 2H_2 + 2O_2 = 2H_2O$$

The overall reaction remains that between hydrogen and oxygen to produce water, as shown above. The processes are shown diagrammatically in Fig. 3.1.

The AFC used by NASA for its Apollo space missions was the first commercial fuel cell. This cell was based closely on the Bacon cell but with some practical revisions to reduce weight. The cell operated at

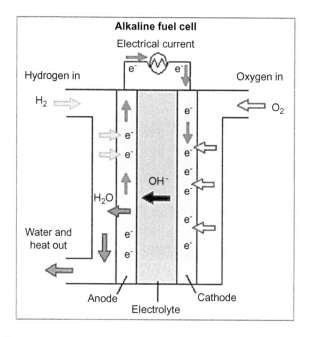

Figure 3.1 The alkaline fuel cell. Source: US Department of Energy.

260°C and just over 3 atmospheres. Electrodes for the cell were also based on Bacon's gas diffusion electrodes. The anode was made from porous nickel while the cathode was oxidized porous nickel. The cell produced a cell voltage of 0.87 V at its operating temperature. In the Apollo space craft, three of these cells were used in parallel. Each cell requires constant heat and water removal to prevent either overheating or waterlogging and this was achieved with hydrogen circulation which swept away the water vapor resulting from water production at the hydrogen anode as well as providing a cooling circuit.

For the later space shuttle AFC, the design was changed significantly. The operating temperature was dropped to 93°C and the pressure raised slightly, to 4 atmospheres, while the concentration of the electrolyte was reduced to 32%. The diffusion electrode design was abandoned in favor of mesh electrodes made from gold plated nickel to which a catalyst layer and Teflon were added. The Teflon provided hydrophobic gas passages through the electrodes. The catalyst at the anode was 20 mg/m^2 of gold/platinum alloy while the cathode carried 10 mg/m^2 of platinum. Meanwhile the electrolyte itself was held within a porous solid matrix of asbestos. The space shuttle fuel cells each provided 7 kW average power and 12 kW peak power and had a life-time or around 2600 h. Three were used in each space vehicle.

3.3 CURRENT AFC DESIGN

While the AFC is potentially one of the most efficient fuel cells available, its practical use has been limited by a number of factors including the absorption of carbon dioxide by the electrolyte leading to the production of carbonate and the corrosion of the cell components as a result of contact with the strong alkali solution. The latter a had a significant impact on the lifetime of the space AFC designs although the lifespan was improved between the Apollo AFC and that used in the space shuttle. Electrolyte poisoning was less of a factor in the space cells because the fuel was pure oxygen.

Catalyst economics are also important. High temperature cells such as Bacon's and the Apollo AFC allow the use of nickel or other non-precious metal electrodes but the electrolyte is more corrosive at the elevated temperatures and system design is more difficult. For terrestrial use, low-temperature cells are preferred but this currently necessitates the use of precious metal catalysts on the electrodes, raising costs. Cheaper catalysts are a primary goal for AFC research.

While cost is an important factor, cell lifetime is probably the most important restriction on AFC applications today. As noted above the AFCs used in the US space program were able to achieve lifetimes of 2600 h[1] and lifetimes of 4000–5000 h appear achievable with modern terrestrial designs. While relatively short, this is considered sufficient for a power unit in a vehicle, potentially allowing a range of 200,000 km. However, much greater lifetimes are normally required for stationary power applications.

Electrolyte poisoning and corrosion are the main culprits reducing the operating lifetime of a cell. Component corrosion can be tacked using barrier layers and by modifying system design to minimize the contact between susceptible components and the electrolyte. Dealing with electrolyte poisoning resulting from the presence of carbon dioxide is more difficult.

---

[1]There are claims of 15,000 h for space program AFCs.

The most basic reaction between the two is that shown below:

$$CO_2 + 2\,KOH = K_2CO_3 + H_2O$$

The reaction produces potassium carbonate, K_2CO_3, and the presence of this carbonate dissolved in the electrolyte has several effects. First, the concentration of hydroxyl ions is reduced, increasing the ohmic resistance across the cell electrolyte and leading to energy losses. Then the carbonate, which is mildly acidic, can also reduce the pH of the electrolyte which has an adverse effect on the reaction kinetics at the cathode where the oxygen reaction takes place. In addition, it has been suggested that the carbonate could precipitate as a solid into the pores of the electrodes, impeding the passage of the gases. However, the carbonate is relatively soluble in the electrolyte and at typical cell operating temperatures there appears to be no such effect. However it could occur at temperatures close to ambient.

The source of the problem, carbon dioxide, is present in air and will remain as a trace presence in oxygen generated from air. It will commonly be found in hydrogen fuel too, so in most situations it is impossible to eliminate it completely. One obvious strategy for limiting its effect on an AFC is to remove as much as possible of the gas from the feed streams. Various types of absorber are available including soda lime absorption and molecular sieve absorbers.

Absorption will reduce the carbon dioxide concentration but will not eliminate it completely so some will reach the electrolyte and react. However, it is technically possible to remove carbonate that has become dissolved in the electrolyte by operating the cell at a very high current density for a short period of time. The effect of this is to create a very low hydroxyl ion concentration around the anode, so that CO_3^{2-} ions then migrate to the electrode instead, where they form carbonic acid, H_2CO_3 by reaction with hydrogen at the electrode. This acid will then be electrolyzed, decomposing into carbon dioxide and hydrogen under the high current conditions and the carbon dioxide is swept away in the hydrogen stream.

The main alternative approach to tackling carbonate formation and extending the cell lifetime is by electrolyte recirculation during which the electrolyte is either replaced or cleaned. A circulating electrolyte AFC can either simply refresh the electrolyte slowly by providing a constant stream of fresh electrolyte at one side of the cell while removing deteriorated electrolyte from the other, or it can use a recirculation system in which the electrolyte is passed through a cleaning system to remove carbonate before being returned to the cell. Circulation of the electrolyte has other advantages besides carbonate removal. It helps with cell cooling and with the management of the water generated within the fuel cell by the fuel cell reaction. It can also assist in keeping an even concentration of electrolyte throughout the cell. Commercial cells with circulation are under development.

3.4 HYDROGEN FUEL FOR AFCs

The normal source of hydrogen for fuel cells today is the reformation of natural gas. The reforming process produces a gas composed primarily of hydrogen and carbon dioxide with small amounts of other impurities such as carbon monoxide, nitrogen, and unreacted methane. It is relatively simple to remove most of the carbon dioxide from this mixture but it becomes more difficult, the purer the hydrogen has to be. In order to meet the requirements of an AFC fuel cell, the cost of purification can become uneconomically high. As a consequence other ways of delivering hydrogen to an AFC fuel cell have been explored.

Hydrazine, N_2H_4, is a chemical source of hydrogen. It will decompose into nitrogen and hydrogen with relative ease and this reaction is highly exothermic. Hydrazine has also been proposed as a direct replacement for hydrogen as the fuel at the anode of an AFC. The fuel can be used in a standard AFC with little modification. The technology to achieve this was tested by the US military during the 1960s and a number of 300 W stacks were produced. However, the material is very unstable and not easy to handle so a hydrazine AFC has not been developed commercially.

Closely related to the hydrazine fuel cell is a hydrazine-hydrogen peroxide fuel cell in which hydrazine is supplied to the anode of a cell and hydrogen peroxide to the cathode. This type of cell could provide a higher efficiency but is more complex than a conventional AFC. It also suffers from the same hydrazine handling problem.

Of more immediate commercial interest is the use of ammonia as the source of hydrogen for an AFC. Ammonia is manufactured globally as a feedstock for chemical plants and so is easily available, and cheap. In its liquid form, it contains more hydrogen per unit of volume that liquid hydrogen, the obvious way to store hydrogen, and it is easily cracked at 500°C to produce hydrogen through the reaction:

$$2NH_3 = N_2 + 3H_2$$

The nitrogen produced in the reaction alongside hydrogen is inert and can pass through the cell without harming it. In addition, the alkaline electrolyte is relatively impervious to the presence of any unreacted ammonia. A European Union funded project called Alkammonia is exploring the potential for ammonia as fuel for an AFC used as a stationary power source.

3.5 HYDROXYL ION EXCHANGE MEMBRANES

AFCs use a liquid electrolyte generally made from potassium hydroxide solution. While this provides a simple and effective cell, the use of a liquid electrolyte also causes technical difficulties. Membranes are much easier to manage and to integrate into cell structures and there are a number of research projects that are seeking to develop a hydroxyl ion exchange membrane that can be used as an electrolyte in place of the liquid hydroxide solution.

The precedent for this type of design is the proton exchange membrane used in acidic electrolyte fuel cells. These cells have proved simple, light, and effective and are being developed for automotive use. The hydroxyl ion exchange membrane would operate in a similar way. In a membrane electrolyte of this type, the active elements, the acidic, or alkaline moieties, are fixed to a polymer chain rather than being free to move in an aqueous solution. Because they are fixed it is impossible for them to react with carbon dioxide and form carbonates. They are also much easier to handle than a liquid electrolyte and cell fabrication can be carried out using techniques such as printing of electrodes and catalysts onto the membrane, techniques that are impossible with liquid electrolytes.

There are limitations, however. The conductivity of a polymer membrane is much lower than it would be for a liquid electrolyte, so a very thin membrane layer must be used. Identifying suitable hydroxyl ion polymeric materials has proved difficult and most show poor chemical stability. Finding a material that can be fabricated simply and in a way consistent with mass production has been a major hurdle too.

However, there is a significant research effort concentrated on finding such membranes and some discoveries in the second decade of the 21st century have shown promise.

3.6 AFCs AND ALTERNATIVE FUELS

While hydrogen is the fuel of choice for most fuel cells there are alternative ways of supplying hydrogen to an AFC that may have distinct advantages. Hydrazine had already been mentioned as fuel to replace pure hydrogen but this material is too hazardous to be of general use.

Another range of materials that are potentially of interest are metal hydrides. Some metals will absorb and store hydrogen within their atomic structure and this hydrogen can then be released in a cell to provide fuel for electricity production. The advantage of this is that the cell can carry it energy source with it and when exhausted, the metal can be refueled with hydrogen. However, these metal hydrides are essentially providing a way of storing hydrogen and do not actively take part in the cell reaction.

Another class of hydrides can be used directly as fuel. These have hydrogen chemically bonded to them. One of the most interesting is sodium borohydride $NaBh_4$. This can react electrochemically in an AFC according to the cell reaction:

$$NaBH_4 + 2O_2 = NaBO_2 + 2H_2O$$

In this way the sodium borohydride will react directly at the cell electrode. This offers a simpler way of providing hydrogen fuel for an AFC. However, the process is complicated by a reaction of the borohydride with water to produce gaseous hydrogen within the cell. More importantly, it has so far proved difficult to recycle sodium borate, $NaBO_2$ back into sodium borohydride.

3.7 APPLICATIONS OF AFCs

The use of AFCs has so far been limited to a few applications where the high efficiency and simplicity of the cell is the most important factor. First among these have been their use in space exploration by both the United States and other countries. However, while the AFCs are one of the best sources of power for sublunar exploration, they are unlikely to be suitable for manned exploration beyond to moon, when nuclear power units are likely to be necessary.

Outside the space program, applications have been restricted to a number of vehicle applications such as fork-lift trucks and golf trolleys. Costs are too high and lifetimes currently too short for their use for general automotive applications but if both could be reduced they would have great potential. This is the focus for much AFC research and development. One company has also been developing an AFC for stationary power applications.

CHAPTER 4

The Proton Exchange Membrane Fuel Cell

The proton exchange membrane (PEM) fuel cell is a fuel cell in which the cell electrolyte is a hydrated polymer instead of the more usual liquid. It takes its name from this polymeric PEM, an acidic membrane that, when saturated with water, will conduct positively charged hydrogen ions—protons—through its structure. A membrane has many advantages over a simple liquid for cell construction including low weight and ease of fabrication. However, its conductivity is relatively low compared to a liquid phase acidic solution. This can lead to a high internal cell resistance but may be overcome by using extremely thin membranes within a cell.

The PEM fuel cell was invented by the US company General Electric (GE) and was initially intended for military applications. Its advantages were soon recognized by NASA and it was used in some early manned space flights. At the same time the light weight cell was also attractive for automotive applications and it was used both at sea, in submarines, and in land-based vehicles. This use has continued to attract investment and the PEM fuel cell is one of the main candidates as a power supply unit for electric vehicles. There has been a parallel development of stationary power applications but here the low weight is less of an advantage whereas overall efficiency is a key factor. The cell is highly efficient when provided with hydrogen fuel but less so when the hydrogen is produced by reforming natural gas.

The polymer membrane that gives the cell its name is constructed from a backbone compound that is a close relative of teflon. This backbone has acidic molecular groups attached to it. In its normal state the membrane will not conduct protons but if it is saturated with water then the acid molecular groups release protons, conveying conductivity via the water within the membrane. As a consequence of the conductivity being conferred by water, the membrane must be kept below the boiling point of water. Normal cells operate at around 80°C. This is a relatively low temperature for a fuel cell and makes its

Fuel Cells. DOI: http://dx.doi.org/10.1016/B978-0-08-101039-6.00004-2

electrode catalyst, which is usually platinum, susceptible to poisoning. Cells can achieve 60% efficiency when operating with pure hydrogen.

4.1 THE HISTORY OF THE PEM FUEL CELL

The PEM fuel cell was developed by US scientists Thomas Grubb and Leonard Niedrach at GE. The first successful cell was announced in 1960. The small cell was developed under a program for the US Navy's Bureau of Ships and the US Army Signal Corps. That cell was fueled with hydrogen which was generated by mixing water with lithium hydride carried in disposable canisters. It required a platinum catalyst but was small and easily portable.

NASA soon identified fuel cells as ideal power sources for manned space flights because they were able to provide water for drinking and cabin humidification as well as generating electrical power. As a consequence, GE was commissioned to provide fuel cells for the Gemini earth-orbiting manned space program. Seven flights between 1962 and 1965 used PEM fuel cells.

The fuel cell designed for the Gemini space craft was a 1 kW power plant with three stacks of 32 cells each. The average power was 620 W. Hydrogen and oxygen were cryogenically cooled and stored in liquid form. The cell operated at 21°C. Cell electrodes were titanium screens carrying a platinum catalyst. The actual membrane in this fuel cell was made from sulfonated polystyrene resin. A similar cell was adopted in 1967 for a biosatellite space craft but in this case the membrane was made from a perfluorosulfonic acid ionomer[1] developed by DuPont under the name Nafion. This is the polymer used in most commercial cells today.

A problem with the Gemini fuel cell was its sensitivity to membrane water content. Either too little or too much water could lead to power loss so the cell was designed with wicks to carry excess water to a ceramic porous separator. The PEM fuel cell technology was replaced by AFC technology for the later Apollo space flights to the moon.

GE continued to develop the PEM technology into the 1970s for US Navy underwater projects and it was adopted by the British Navy

---

[1]An ionomer is a polymer where the molecular components are held together by ionic bonding rather than the more usual molecular bonds.

for its submarine fleet in the 1980s. Other companies began to take interest too while in the late 1980s in the United States the Los Almos National Laboratory and Texas A&M University both launched research programs to try and reduce the amount of platinum required for PEM catalysts. In the 1990s a Canadian company Ballard Systems tested PEM fuel cells in buses and the company also explored their use in stationary applications. Other companies have since taken up the technology and stationary applications now include both large utility sized stationary fuel cell stacks and small ones for domestic applications. Alongside this, many of the world's automotive companies are investing in PEM fuel cells as potential vehicle power units where their low mass makes them attractive.

4.2 THE PEM PRINCIPLE

The PEM fuel cell exploits the reaction between hydrogen and oxygen typical of most fuel cells. The electrolyte of the cell is an acidic polymer membrane that is permeable to protons and it is the transfer of protons from one electrode of the cell to the other across the membrane that permits the reaction to proceed. The cell is shown diagrammatically in Fig. 4.1.

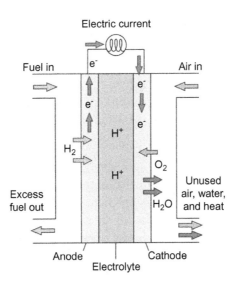

Figure 4.1 The PEM fuel cell. Source: Wikipedia Commons.

The reaction can be broken down into two half reactions, one taking place at each electrode of the cell. Hydrogen supplied to the anode is absorbed onto the platinum catalyst where the molecular hydrogen dissociates into atoms and then each atom gives up an electron to the electrode and passes into the electrolyte solution as a positively charged hydrogen atom, a proton. Meanwhile at the cathode, oxygen is absorbed onto the electrode surface where it too dissociates into oxygen atoms. Each atom then takes two electrons, electrons that have passed from the cathode through the external circuit, to form negatively charged oxygen ions. These react with protons that have migrated through the electrolyte from the anode to the cathode, forming molecules of water. The sequence of half-cell reactions and the full reaction are shown below.

$$\text{Anode reaction: } 2H_2 = 4H^+ + 4e^-$$

$$\text{Cathode reaction: } O_2 + 4H^+ + 4e^- = 2H_2O$$

$$\text{Overall cell reaction: } 2H_2 + O_2 = 2H_2O$$

The membrane which forms the electrolyte of the PEM cell is typically a compound called poly-perfluorocarbon sulfonate. This is a close relative of teflon but with acidic sulfonate molecular groups attached to its polymer backbone which provide conductivity when the membrane is hydrated. In its normal state the membrane is not conductive but if it is allowed to become saturated with water the acidic groups attached to the membrane release protons, allowing it to conduct hydrogen ions. The membrane itself is usually between 50 μm and 175 μm thick, the latter equivalent to seven sheets of paper. As a consequence of the fact that the conductivity is provided by water, the cell must be kept well below the boiling point if it is to remain stable. Practical cells normally operate at around 80°C.

The operation of the PEM cell is extremely sensitive to its water content. The cell reaction produces water at the cathode and this must be carried away from the cell otherwise the cell might flood, preventing the hydrogen and oxygen gases from reaching the electrodes. This is usually achieved by using excess air to carry away the water which is produced in liquid form at the lower operating temperature of the cell. However, it is important to prevent too much water being carried away during operation as this impairs performance too, so the incoming gas streams are usually humidified.

The low operating temperature of the PEM cell means that the cell reaction must be catalyzed using platinum in order for it to proceed sufficiently rapidly to make the cell viable. Even with the catalyst, the speed of the oxygen reaction at the cathode is often the limiting factor in cell operation.

The use of a membrane electrolyte makes construction of a PEM fuel cell relatively simple compared to that of other types of fuel cell. The electrodes of the cell are normally made from a fine carbon particles that have been coated with the precious metal catalyst. These coated particles can be applied to the membrane directly using a printing technique or by using direct deposition similar to that used for microchip construction. However from a manufacturing perspective, it is often considered simpler to construct separate cathode and anode structures, usually based on porous carbon, and then bond these to the membrane to form the cell.

A complete membrane and electrode assembly will be around 200 μm thick. A backing layer of porous carbon, often treated with teflon to prevent waterlogging, is then applied to each electrode. These backing layers, which are typically 100−300 μm thick, serve multiple functions. They add strength to the cell assembly, they act as current collectors and they provide a porous layer through which hydrogen and oxygen can reach the electrodes and water can be removed. A typical cell structure in shown in Fig. 4.2. Metal current collectors and gas flow systems are then bonded to each backing layer. In practical systems cells are stacked one on top of the other to provide a higher voltage. In these stacks one metal collector can be used to contact the anode of one cell and the cathode of a second.

The cell voltage from a PEM cell is 0.7−0.8 V at full power. A typical cell will provide around 0.6 A for each square centimeter. A commercial cell may have an active area of up to 200 cm^2, potentially providing a current of around 120 A and a power of 80−100 W.

The lifetime of a PEM fuel cell is typically around 10,000 h. This is low for many stationary applications where operational lifetimes of 10−20 years (90,000−180,000 h) are common for other technologies, but may be sufficient for automotive applications where a lifetime of 4000 h has been considered adequate. Some recent cells have claimed lifetimes of 40,000 h which would be suitable for some stationary applications where intermittent rather than continuous use is required.

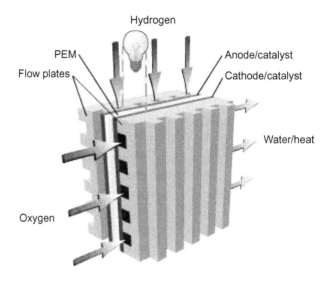

Figure 4.2 A practical PEM fuel cell structure. Source: Wikipedia Commons.

4.3 PEM FUEL CELL CATALYSTS

The low operating temperature of a conventional PEM fuel cell necessitates that it use an excellent catalyst at the electrodes to facilitate the electrode reactions. The best known and most effective catalyst for these reactions is the precious metal platinum. In commercial cells today the metal is deposited as particles onto porous carbon supports to create the electrodes. Platinum is expensive and so one of the keys to reducing the cost of PEM fuel cells is to reduce the amount of platinum required at each electrode.

The fuel cells in the Gemini space craft, which operated at around ambient temperature, had catalyst loadings of 28 mg/cm^2 of platinum. This is considered a very high catalyst loading today but was needed at the low operating temperature. Early terrestrial fuel cells from the 1960s operating at a more typical 80°C, used lower catalysts loadings of up to 4 mg/cm^2 of platinum at each electrode. This has been reduced in the intervening period so that the typical loading today would be 0.2–0.8 mg/cm^2. However, even these loadings are considered too high for commercial use, particularly in vehicles, and the target of current research is to try and reduce this by a factor of three to four.

Various routes are being explored in an effort to decrease the amount of platinum needed, including attempts to increase the activity of the platinum. One possibility way of achieving, this is to use nano-scale particles of platinum. These small particles provide a very high surface area to mass ratio, an advantageous property when the activity of the platinum takes place on its surface. High activity may also be achieved by depositing platinum onto tiny carbon particles. Another area being explored is the alloying of the platinum with other metals.

The alternative is to try and identify catalysts to replace platinum that use cheaper materials. Some metal/nitrogen/carbon catalytic materials have shown promise but none can yet compete with platinum in terms of activity.

The other problem with platinum in PEM fuel cells is its susceptibility to poisoning. This is much more severe with low temperature cells that those operating at higher temperatures. The two most serious poisons encountered in PEM fuel cells are carbon monoxide and sulfur compounds such as hydrogen sulfide or sulfur dioxide. These sulfur compounds can occur in natural gas, the normal precursor to hydrogen for fuel cells today, and the gas must be scrupulously cleaned to prevent the sulfur reaching the catalyst. Sulfur removal is carried out routinely before natural gas is piped and the danger from sulfur poisoning is generally low.

Much more serious is the susceptibility to carbon monoxide poisoning. At the normal operating temperature the tolerance of a PEM fuel cell to carbon monoxide is less than 50 parts per million and in practice levels much lower than this will be sought. Carbon monoxide is a particular problem because it is a product of the reforming of natural gas, and a normal impurity in hydrogen generated in this way. Therefore PEM fuel cell research is also focussed on finding ways of reducing the carbon monoxide sensitivity. The most effective research of this type is looking at means to remove carbon monoxide from hydrogen before it is fed into the fuel cell. There are some catalysts that will convert the carbon monoxide to carbon dioxide. However, the best future solution is likely to be to produce hydrogen in another way, such as from the electrolysis of water.

An alternative solution is to operate the cells at a higher temperature since this reduces catalyst sensitivity to poisoning. This has led to the development of some higher temperature membranes that have greater tolerance to carbon monoxide. These are discussed below.

4.4 MEMBRANES

While most PEM fuel cells utilize the teflon related material poly-perfluorocarbon sulfonate as their membrane, the operating temperature of this fuel cell membrane is limited to below 100°C due to the presence of water which provides the proton conductivity. Operating at a higher temperature has several advantages. The cell reaction kinetics are accelerated as the temperature rises, making the electrode reactions quicker and an elevated temperature reduces the sensitivity of the catalyst to poisoning. In addition, a higher operating temperature can allow heat to be extracted from the cell for cogeneration applications such as space heating or hot water.

There are a range of PEM fuel cell membranes that have been developed to operate at higher temperatures. The most successful of these are based on polybenzimidazole, a polymer with an exceptionally high heat resistance that is stable at temperatures of up to 400°C. When formed into a membrane, this material can be doped with phosphoric acid. This acid can itself provide the proton conductivity normally supplied by hydrating a membrane with water. Membranes made of polybenzimidazole can also be doped with sulfuric acid.

The polybenzimidazole fuel cell membrane appears to be stable to 220°C and cells have been tested successfully at 160−180°C. In these cells the proton conductivity does not rely on water and so water management becomes easier. These high temperature PEM fuel cells can tolerate 1%−5% by volume of carbon monoxide in the hydrogen fuel but they are less tolerant to some other impurities and they have lower power densities than the traditional low temperature Nafion membrane version. As a consequence, this type of membrane is unlikely to replace the traditional PEM but there may particular low power density applications for which it is better suited.

4.5 NATURAL GAS REFORMING

The PEM fuel cell requires hydrogen fuel to be supplied to its anode in order to generate electricity. In most cases this will be provided by reforming natural gas. Commercial fuel cells' systems for stationary applications based on PEM fuel cells will usually include a reformer as part of the package.

Reforming is a two stage process. The first stage is called steam reforming. Steam reforming is carried out by mixing the natural gas with high temperature steam at 800−1000°C and passing the mixture over a catalyst at a pressure of between 3 bar and 25 bar. The main constituent of natural gas is methane and this reacts with water according to the equation below to produce a mixture of hydrogen and carbon monoxide, a product which is known as synthesis gas.

$$CH_4 + H_2O = CO + 3H_2$$

Synthesis gas is widely used industrially during the manufacture of chemicals. It contains a large proportion of carbon monoxide and so cannot be used directly as fuel for a PEM fuel cell. However, the carbon monoxide can be removed by a further reaction, the water-shift reaction. During this reaction, which is shown below, the synthesis gas is mixed with more steam and again passed over a catalyst at high temperature.

$$CO + H_2O = CO_2 + H_2$$

During the water-shift reaction, the carbon monoxide reacts with the water to produce carbon dioxide and more hydrogen. The overall reformer reaction, when both processes are combined, is as shown below.

$$CH_4 + 2H_2O = CO_2 + 4H_2$$

The reactions above are for methane but other hydrocarbons found in natural gas will react in a similar way.

Since carbon monoxide is one of the products of the reforming reaction, there are always traces left in the final gas, even after carrying out the water-shift reaction. This must be scrupulously removed in order to prevent platinum poisoning. Typically, a carbon monoxide concentration of below 10 ppm is required in the fuel for a low temperature PEM fuel cell.

While natural gas is the most common source of hydrogen for fuel cells, there are other sources that can be used, including methanol and gasoline. Methanol undergoes a similar steam reforming reaction to natural gas, usually carried out at around 200°C, producing a mixture of hydrogen and carbon monoxide which is then converted to more hydrogen with a water-shift reaction. A similar process can be carried out using gasoline but a higher temperature, 800°C is required.

In order to simplify the production of hydrogen for a PEM fuel cell, research is underway to develop a reformer capable of operating with a variety of input fuels. This type of reformer will be important if PEM fuel cells are to be used in vehicles. A fuel cell with this type of reformer built into it is called a reformate fuel cell.

Steam reforming and the water-shift reaction are both energy intensive. The heat required to carry out the processes is normally supplied by burning some of the natural gas that will eventually provide hydrogen for the fuel cell. This drops the overall efficiency of the power generation process. In theory a PEM fuel cell can operate at 60% fuel to electrical efficiency when fed pure hydrogen although in practice the efficiency is likely to be lower. However, when provided with hydrogen from a reformer, the overall efficiency drops to around 42%. A reformer for a PEM fuel cell also requires around 20 m to start-up and reach its operating temperature. When operated with pure hydrogen no warm up is required.

4.6 COMMERCIAL APPLICATIONS OF PEM FUEL CELLS

There are a range of stationary applications for PEM fuel cells but they have yet to establish themselves in any one part of the market. Early development was directed at large stationary cell stacks with capacities of up to 250 kW and there has been one 1 MW utility application. However, the largest units today are likely to be below 100 kW. Meanwhile, many companies are developing much smaller units. One of the important potential uses is for domestic combined heat and power, with the fuel cell providing both electricity and low grade heat for hot water and space heating.

Smaller PEM fuel cells are being used for backup and standby power. Another application that is growing in popularity is for portable power generation. These units take advantage of the high efficiency of the PEM fuel cell when operating with hydrogen to provide a cheap, highly efficient source of portable power. This is a market that is also being addressed by the direct methanol fuel cell (see Chapter 8).

Much of the pioneering work on the PEM fuel cell was carried out in the United States and Canada, but in recent years Japanese companies have also taken a strong interest. Japan is home to an active domestic fuel cell program at which a number of products are directed. PEM units of around 750 W are being installed in homes in Japan under a government-backed program. In Europe interest is mostly for small PEM fuels for portable and standby power as well as for domestic use.

In the middle of the second decade of the 21st century PEM fuel cells accounted for the largest number of fuel cells sold annually both in terms of numbers and in terms of capacity shipped by manufacturers. A large part of these sales are due to the introduction of the first electric vehicles with fuel cells which arrived on the market in 2015.

CHAPTER 5

The Phosphoric Acid Fuel Cell

The phosphoric acid fuel cell (PAFC) takes its name from the acid that serves as its electrolyte. Phosphoric acid, H_3PO_4, is a solid at room temperature but melts at 42°C. The material is not an obvious candidate for a fuel cell electrolyte but was found to have several beneficial properties that made it suitable for development.

The acid is stable up to around 200°C, allowing a fuel cell based on this material to operate at a higher temperature than the proton exchange membrane (PEM) fuel cell and reducing sensitivity to carbon monoxide poisoning. The high temperature also accelerates the electrode reactions. Early development work on the PAFC started in the 1960s and its promise led to government support in the United States. Japanese companies also become involved in the development of the technology, and in the 1990s the PAFC became the first fuel cell system to be offered commercially for terrestrial stationary power applications. Since then a limited range of fuel cells based on this electrolyte have been available, mainly for stationary power and combined heat and power.

Fuel cell systems based on the PAFC are normally designed to operate with natural gas although other fuels including biogas can be used. They require an external reformer to convert the fuel gas into hydrogen. The operating temperature of the cells is high enough that waste heat can be captured and used to provide space heating and hot water and many PAFC systems are designed as combined heat and power plants. As a result of their almost silent operation and low emissions, they can be used in sensitive urban areas where other types of generator might be less suitable.

The PAFC is less efficient than several other types of fuel cell but the commercial systems that have been developed have proved robust and they remain popular for medium capacity stationary applications in the 100−500 kW range, particularly in Asia and the United States.

Fuel Cells. DOI: http://dx.doi.org/10.1016/B978-0-08-101039-6.00005-4

5.1 HISTORY OF THE PAFC

Interest in the PAFC started in the early 1960s when two chemists, GV Elmore and HA Tanner, published results of experiments they had conducted using phosphoric acid as the electrolyte in a fuel cell. The two scientists operated a cell for 6 months at 0.25 V, at a current density of 90 mA/cm^2, without sign of deterioration.

Phosphoric acid is a poor conductor but it is not reduced electrochemically during cell operation, an advantage compared to other acidic electrolytes that had been tried. Acids are potential electrolytes because they will conduct the protons that are a key mediator in many fuel cell reactions. In addition, Elmore and Tanner found that a phosphoric acid cell can operate using air rather than pure oxygen. To construct the cell they mixed the acid with silica power and the resulting paste was loaded into a teflon gasket, then electrodes applied.

The results of this experimental work spurred research into phosphoric acid and the US Army took an early interest in the PAFC because it could operate with "logistical fuels" that were readily available to troops in the field. It tested a unit built by Allis Chalmers with fuel supplied from a steam reformer from Engelhard Industries.

Development progressed during the 1960s and 1970s, supported by an industry partnership called the Team to Advance Research for Gas Energy Transformation (TARGET) which was funded by Pratt and Whitney and the American Gas Association. By 1969 fuel cells with a capacity of 15 kW were being tested; in 1983 the capacity had reached 5 MW. The Japanese utility Tokyo Gas became a member of TARGET in 1972, starting a Japanese interest in the PAFC fuel cell that has continued since that time.

Further sponsorship by US organizations including the US Department of Energy and the US Gas Institute as well as gas and electric utilities led finally to the development of a commercial fuel cell by company called ONSI, a subsidiary of International Fuel Corp, which was itself a joint venture between Toshiba and United Technologies Corp. (UTC)—the latter the parent of Pratt and Whitney. The system was launched in 1992. It had an electrical output of 200 kW and provided 220 kW of heat. Around 200 of these units were installed across the world. The largest installation was a 1 MW plant using five units that supplied power to a postal sorting office in Alaska. Meanwhile development advanced in Japan too, with Fuji Electric Co and Mitsubishi Electric Co launching commercial products which were also marketed during the 1990s. During that decade PAFCs were also tested in vehicles including buses. Since then new units have been developed with capacities of up to 400 kW and these remain available commercially.

5.2 THE PAFC PRINCIPLE

The PAFC uses an acid electrolyte to exploit the reaction between hydrogen and oxygen in an electrochemical cell to produce electrical power. The electrolyte is pure phosphoric acid which is a solid at room temperature but melts at $42°C$ and is stable in liquid form to just above $200°C$. It is a proton conductor, with a relatively low overall conductivity. To overcome this, the electrolyte is normally loaded into an inert matrix so that it forms a thin wafer between the electrodes. Catalysts are applied to the electrodes to accelerate the cell reactions.

In the cell, hydrogen is supplied to the anode where the molecules of the gas are absorbed onto the surface of the electrode and then dissociate, leaving hydrogen atoms which give up electrons and pass into the electrolyte as protons. The protons can cross the cell through the phosphoric acid to reach the cathode where oxygen from air is also absorbed onto the electrode and the molecules dissociate, then the oxygen atoms take two electrons from the external circuit to form ions which react with protons migrating from the anode to make water (see Fig. 5.1). These reactions, which are exactly the same as those described for the PEM fuel cell in Chapter 4, are shown below.

$$\text{Anode reaction: } 2H_2 = 4H^+ + 4e^-$$

$$\text{Cathode reaction: } O_2 + 4H^+ + 4e^- = 2H_2O$$

$$\text{Overall cell reaction: } 2H_2 + O_2 = 2H_2O$$

In practical modern cells the electrolyte is held in a teflon-bonded silicon carbide matrix. It is a liquid at the cell operating temperature which is typically between $150°C$ and $200°C$ and is held in position within the matrix by capillary action. In its liquid form it can evaporate, or migrate, and so care must be taken to control electrolyte loss to maintain cell activity. A PAFC cell is usually operated at atmospheric pressure but they can be operated at higher pressure. This can

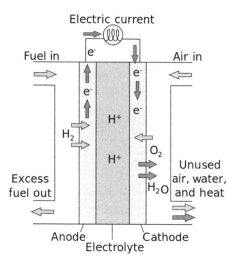

Figure 5.1 The phosphoric acid fuel cell. Source: Wikipedia commons.

increase overall efficiency but at the expense of higher cell component corrosion rates as the acid reactivity increases.

The electrodes of a PAFC cell are made from porous carbon paper to which a catalyst is applied. The latter is normally platinum or a platinum alloy. The oxygen reaction at the cathode is the limiting factor in cell operation and this electrode requires a higher catalyst loading to speed the process. The cathode catalyst is usually pure platinum. The anode catalyst is often a platinum—ruthenium alloy. The latter aids the oxidation of carbon monoxide impurity from the reformer into carbon dioxide, reducing the potential for catalyst poisoning. The electrodes are bonded to the electrolyte matrix using teflon mounts.

The electrode structure is designed to permit the fuel gases to be fed into the electrodes and the porous carbon is conducting and acts as a current collector. The cell voltage in a PAFC fuel cell is typically 0.65 V. To increase the voltage, individual cells are usually stacked back to back, in series, with the anode of one cell connected directly to the cathode of the next. The conductivity of the carbon electrodes assists in making this series connection between cells by conducting electrical power from one cell to the next.

Water is produced at the cell cathode and this must be removed to prevent the water from dissolving in the electrolyte and affecting cell performance. Removal is achieved by passing excess air through the cathode to carry the water away as water vapor. Commercial cells operate at as close to 200°C as possible to maximize the kinetics at the cathode and to increase the carbon monoxide tolerance of the cell. At this operating temperature the water is produced in the gaseous state so this can be carried away easily by the air feed to the cathode. Above 200°C the electrolyte may start to decompose as well as becoming increasingly reactive towards the carbon in the electrodes so this is the upper operating temperature limit.

Cells must be heated from cold start before they can be operated but once they reach operating point, the cell produces more than sufficient heat to maintain the required temperature. Excess heat must be removed during operation. The can be achieved using either liquid or gaseous coolants. Liquids tend to be more efficient but the cooling systems are more complex than with gases. In many systems this waste heat is captured and used for heating or hot water. The heat is also used to drive the reformer that produces hydrogen for the fuel cell, usually from natural gas.

For normal operation, the carbon monoxide level must be kept below 1.5% by volume to minimize poisoning. Sulfur tolerance is virtually zero so all sulfur compounds must be scrupulously removed.

Practical PAFC fuel cells have fuel to electrical conversion efficiencies of between 36% and 42%. The higher efficiencies are achieved in cells operating under greater than atmospheric pressure. With combined heat and power utilization where waste heat is captured and reused, the overall efficiency can reach 87%. PAFC cells have shown lifetimes of up to 40,000 h and development is expected to extend this further. The cells can operate under a wide range of atmospheric conditions and commercial cells have operated at temperatures as low as −32°C and has high as 87°C.

5.3 FUEL PROCESSING

A PAFC requires pure hydrogen to be supplied to the anode. Since this is not generally available commercially, most PAFCs rely on the reforming of natural gas to provide their fuel. This process, described in Chapter 4, involves reacting the natural gas at high temperature with steam to produce a mixture that is mainly composed of hydrogen and carbon dioxide. This process is energy intensive and reduces the efficiency of the PAFC since some energy from the fuel must be used to drive the reformation reactions. Commercial PAFCs will normally include an integrated reformer that simply needs connecting to a gas supply in order to the system to operate.

The amount of carbon dioxide produced during steam reforming of natural gas is the same as would have been produced if the gas had been burnt in air in a gas turbine or steam plant. The use of the reforming means, therefore, that the PAFC still produces significant quantities of carbon dioxide which will normally be released into the atmosphere. It is, in principle, possible to capture the carbon dioxide either after reforming, or after hydrogen has been burnt in the fuel cell. However, this is not a commercial option today. The operating temperature of the PAFC is very low compared to that of a combustion plant and there are no nitrogen oxides produced. As already noted, the natural gas must be cleaned to remove any sulfur compounds or these would poison the platinum catalyst, so there are no sulfur emissions either.

In addition to natural gas, there are other fuels that can be used to supply hydrogen to a PAFC. These include gas generated by anaerobic digestion of waste material, which produces a methane rich biogas. It is possible to make hydrogen from coal too, though that is unlikely to be an economical means of supplying fuel to a small fuel cell installation.

5.4 COMMERCIAL CELLS

The development of PAFCs has taken place mostly in either the United States or Japan. The earliest commercial unit was launched by ONSI in 1992. Other companies that have a long history of PAFC cell development are Fuji Electric Corp. and Mitsubishi Electric Corp.

The first commercial PAFC to reach the market was called the PC25C. The unit had an electrical output of 200 kW. It was designed to operate on natural gas and consumed 58 m^3/h at its nominal output. Nominal electrical efficiency was 40% and the combined heat and power efficiency, with heat recovered for hot water and heating, was 87%. Thermal output was 260 kW. Around 200 of these units were installed in the United States, Europe, and Asia; the largest installation included five units providing 1 MW of power to a post office facility in

Alaska. The catalyst in these original systems had to be replaced every 5 years.

In the first decade of the 21st century the ONSI fuel cell was rebranded as the PureCell and two sizes, 200 and 400 kW were available. Twelve of the larger units have been installed in the Freedom Tower in New York, built on the site of the former World Trade Center. These units provide 4.8 MW of electrical energy as well as supplying heat. The technology was acquired by Doosan in 2014, and this company is now manufacturing the PureCell units.

Japanese interest in PAFC technology begin 1992 when the utility Tokyo Electric joined the TARGET research project. The utility tested a range of fuel cell units including a 40 kW and a 200 kW unit manufactured by ONSI. Between 1991 and 1997 the utility was home to a 11 MW PAFC that operated for over 23,000 h and recorded a gross electrical efficiency of 44%. The utility was also involved in a domestic venture to develop PAFC technology, and since 1986 it has worked in conjunction with Fuji Electric. The latter developed two units, at 50 and 100 kW, and by the middle of the first decade of the 21st century more than 90 units had been installed and operated.

Fuji Electric continues to manufacture PAFCs. It now offers a 100 kW unit with an electrical efficiency of 42% and a combined heat and power efficiency of 91%. A key area of development in Japan has been cell lifetime, and the current generation can operate for more than 60,000 h.

The PAFC remains the most mature commercial fuel cell and still retains and important share of the market for stationary power applications. Its main market is to supply power to small commercial organizations or to facilities such as hospitals and universities where both heat and power can be utilized. Unit sizes of 100−400 kW are the most economical and this too defines the areas in which these fuel cells offer most appeal.

CHAPTER 6

The Molten Carbonate Fuel Cell

The molten carbonate fuel cell (MCFC) is the most complex of all the modern fuel cells both in terms of its cell reaction and of cell construction. It is a high-temperature cell, operating at around 650°C and its electrolyte is a mixture of alkali metal carbonates that are solid at room temperature but liquid at the cell operating temperature. The high temperature and the use of a molten salt present significant engineering challenges but the cell is theoretically capable of very high efficiency. In addition, the high temperature offers the opportunity of a hybrid configuration that can increase efficiency still further, though with much added complexity.

Research into high-temperature fuel cells began into the 1930s but it was not until the 1950s that a cell was operated successfully for an extended period. During the 1960s the US army began to look at the technology, and in the 1970s the US Department of Energy started to fund research. Full commercialization did not take place until the first decade of the current century. The complexity of the MCFC means that it is only economical in relatively large sizes.

High-temperature fuel cells have several advantages. These include a much lower susceptibility to poisoning by carbon monoxide, the ability to carry out reformation within the cell itself and the availability of high-quality heat that can be used to generate more power or to provide heat for industrial processes, hot water or space heating. In addition the cell reactions take place much more readily at the higher operating temperature than in lower temperature cells, so there is no need for the expensive precious metal catalysts to accelerate the processes.

6.1 THE HISTORY OF THE MCFC

The first research into high-temperature fuel cells took place during the 1930s in Switzerland. At that time the focus was on solid oxide electrolytes but low electrical conductivity and unwanted side reactions

Fuel Cells. DOI: http://dx.doi.org/10.1016/B978-0-08-101039-6.00006-6

hindered progress. Work in Russia a decade later ran into similar problems. During the 1950s two scientists in the Netherlands, GHJ Broers and JAA Ketelaar, took up the subject but switched their attention to high-temperature liquid electrolytes and their work soon focussed on molten carbonate salts. In 1960 they reported work on a cell with an electrolyte that was composed of a mixture of lithium, sodium, and potassium carbonates that ran for 6 months. The electrolyte was held in a porous disk of solid magnesium oxide. The cell deteriorated over time as electrolyte material was lost, partly through a reaction with the gasket material used to seal the cell.

The research into MCFCs attracted the attention of the US Army and during the 1960s its Mobility Equipment Research and Development Center tested MCFCs manufactured by Texas Instruments. The units ranged in size from 100 to 1000 W. They were designed to operate using "combat gasoline" that was supplied to an external reformer. The insensitivity to carbon monoxide poisoning meant that readily available fuels could easily be used to generate hydrogen, so special fuels were not required.

Development in the United States continued during the 1970s as a result of the US Department of Energy (DOE) instituting a research program involving two industrial partners, M-C Power Corp. and Energy Research Corp., that was eventually to lead to the first major commercial MCFC. This research program continued into the 1990s, and in 1997 M-C Power Corp installed a 250 kW MCFC demonstration unit at a US airforce base which generated 160 MWh of power. The company began to develop a new 75 kW fuel cell stack, with ambitions to scale it up to 300 kW but ceased trading in 2000, and its fuel cell technology was transferred to the US Gas Research Institute.

Alongside this, Energy Research Corp, in 1996–97, installed and operated a 2 MW MCFC in California in a demonstration project sponsored by the US DOE and the Electric Power Research Institute. The company changed its name to FuelCell Energy in 1999 and early in the next decade developed the first commercial units based on the technology.

Japanese companies became interested in MCFC technology at an early stage too and by the early 1990s Ishikawajima Heavy Industries had operated a 1000 W MCFC continuously for 10,000 h. The work was carried out with the support of the Japanese New Energy and Industrial Development Organization, and in 2000 the company work started on commercial development with plans for four 300 kW demonstration units. However by the second decade of the 21st century, development in Japan appeared to have lapsed and no commercial systems are available. Development also took place in South Korea and this continues, with commercial units now available.

6.2 THE MCFC PRINCIPLE

The MCFC has the most complex fuel cell reaction of all the cells available commercially. The electrolyte is a mixture of alkali metal carbonates (typically 62% lithium carbonate and 38% potassium carbonate by molecular proportions, a eutectic[1] which melts at 550°C) which is heated to between 600°C and 1000°C and in its molten state is capable of conducting carbonate ions (CO_3^{2-}). The molten carbonate mixture is held by capillary action within a solid ceramic matrix which is commonly made from lithium aluminum oxide ($LiAlO_2$, also known as lithium aluminate).

Under operating conditions, hydrogen is fed to the anode of the cell where it is absorbed onto the electrode surface and dissociates into hydrogen atoms which then react with carbonate ions in the electrolyte according to the equation:

$$2H_2 + 2CO_3^{2-} = 2H_2O + 2CO_2 + 4e^-$$

During this reaction, part of the electrolyte is consumed and carbon dioxide is released as a gas, mixing with the exhaust stream from the anode. This carbon dioxide must be mixed with air and directed back to the cathode where it reacts with oxygen that has been absorbed onto the cathode and dissociated into atoms, regenerating carbonate ions in the electrolyte according to the reaction:

$$O_2 + 2CO_2 + 4e^- = 2CO_3^{2-}$$

These carbonate ions can then migrate back to the anode, completing the reaction cycle. The overall reaction when these two electrode reactions are taken together is simply that of hydrogen and oxygen as

[1]A eutectic is a mixture of two or more compounds with a specific composition that has a fixed melting point, often lower than either of the components alone or any other mixture.

in other fuel cells but as the chemical equations show it is mediated by the carbonate ions in the electrolyte. A schematic showing the processes taking place in an MCFC are shown in Fig. 6.1.

The normal supply of hydrogen for an MCFC, reformed natural gas, usually contains some carbon monoxide which is a catalyst poison in low temperature cells. In this cell, in contrast, carbon monoxide in the hydrogen fuel can react at the anode to generate more hydrogen via a shift reaction.

$$CO + H_2O = CO_2 + H_2$$

In principle carbon monoxide can also react with carbonate ions at the anode, and can therefore form an alternative fuel for the cell. In practice this latter reaction does not play a significant role in the generation of electricity. However, the insensitivity of the MCFC to carbon monoxide poisoning confers a significant advantage compared to lower temperature cells such as the PEMFC and the PAFC.

The high operating temperature of the cell means that the cell reaction takes place without the need for an expensive platinum catalyst

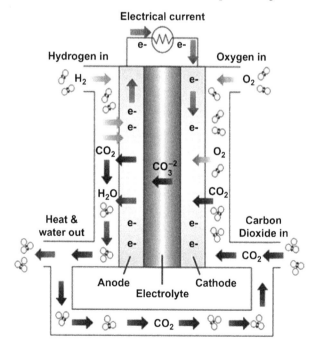

Figure 6.1 The molten carbonate fuel cell. Source: US Department of Energy.

and cheaper, nickel-based electrodes are normally employed. The anode is generally a metallic nickel alloy such as nickel chromium or nickel aluminum while the cathode is nickel oxide. The latter will dissolve slowly in the hot carbonate electrolyte and this can limit cell life. These electrodes are applied to the outer surfaces of the refractory porous tile in which the electrolyte is held. Once the tile is heated, the electrolyte melts and provides the carbonate ion conductivity need for the cell to operate.

The electrolyte, once in liquid form, is held in place by surface forces within the minute pore structure of the refractory tile. However, conditions must be carefully controlled to ensure that the electrolyte, the catalyst and the gases supplied to the electrode are in contact over as large an area as possible. The operating temperature is normally maintained at the minimum compatible will good cell performance. Electrolyte loss takes place slowly through evaporation but this will accelerate, the higher the temperature. A cross-section of a practical cell is shown in Fig. 6.2.

The operating temperature of the MCFC is high enough for the reforming of natural gas to be carried out internally using simple nickel-based catalysts. This allows the reformer to be built into the fuel cell and it is possible for natural gas reforming to take place at the cell

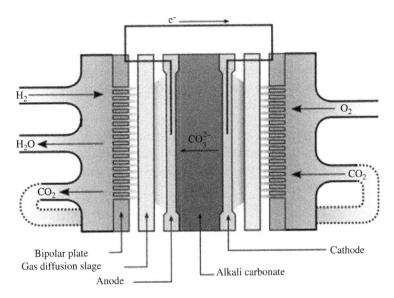

Figure 6.2 Cross-section of a MCFC. Source: Wikipedia commons.

electrodes themselves. This is another major advantage compared to low temperature cells.

Cell voltage is 0.8 V. In order to provide a higher voltage, cells are stacked in series. Each cell must be sealed from the next to prevent cathode and anode gases mixing and this presents complex high-temperature engineering challenges, particularly to find gaskets and seals that will resist the corrosive effects of the electrolyte.

The reason why such a complex cell has proved worth developing lies in the potential efficiency. The theoretical conversion efficiency is 60% although current production units only achieve an efficiency of around 50%. Even so, this efficiency is higher than any simple cycle fossil fuel thermal plant can achieve. These figures do not represent the efficiency limit, however. A MCFC operates a sufficiently high temperature that the fuel or exhaust gases in the cell can also drive a gas turbine, allowing the construction of a hybrid power plants. For greatest efficiency this requires the cell to be pressurized but in this configuration the MCFC may be theoretically capable of between 75% and 80% overall efficiency. Alternatively the high-grade heat produced by the cell can be used for cogeneration or to provide heat for an industrial process.

A further potential advantage of the MCFC is that it can be adapted to capture carbon dioxide produced from reformation of fossil fuels. The cathode of the cell consumes carbon dioxide; if this is supplied from the flue gas of fossil fuel power plant then the carbon dioxide in the flue gases will be consumed. Meanwhile, at the anode carbon dioxide is generated and this can relatively easily be separated and captured, simplifying the carbon capture cycle. Whether such a cycle would be cost effective has yet to be determined.

The relative complexity of the MCFC means that it is not economical to manufacture and operate very small units. Most of the units that have been developed are over 100 kW in capacity and many are two or three times that size.

6.3 HYBRID POWER SYSTEMS

The high-temperature fuel cell offers the potential to combine a thermodynamic heat engine with an electrochemical cell in order to gain higher efficiency. This is possible because the high-temperature fuel cell operates as a sufficiently high temperature that the gases entering or exiting the fuel cell can also be used to drive a turbine.

The best known hybrid MCFC system involves the addition of a microturbine. The latter is a small gas turbine. In this type of system the fuel cell will normally be operated at a pressure higher than atmospheric in order to gain the greatest advantage from adding a small turbine. In this configuration the anode of the MCFC is supplied with hydrogen from a natural gas reformer. Meanwhile the air supplied to the cathode is first pressurized by passing it through the compressor stage of the microturbine. The pressurized air is heated during its passage through the high-temperature fuel cell. Once oxygen has been extracted from the air in the fuel cell, the high-temperature exhaust gas is passed through the turbine stage of the microturbine where its expansion generates energy both to drive the compressor stage of the turbine and to produce electrical energy from a small generator.

The exhaust from the microturbine stills contain significant heat energy. This can be used to produce steam from water to supply the reformer that provides the fuel cell with hydrogen. With close integration of the components, it should be possible to achieve a high-efficiency generating system. Theoretical efficiencies as high as 80% have been mooted although practical efficiencies are likely to be significantly lower. FuelCell Energy and the Italian company Ansaldo have both tested systems of this type.

6.4 FUEL REFORMING

As with most fuel cells the MCFC requires hydrogen at its anode, and this is normally supplied by reforming a fuel such as natural gas. However, as already noted, the high temperature inside the fuel cell means that reforming can easily be carried out internally using a simple nickel catalyst rather than a more complex catalyst that might be required at lower temperature.

It is possible to carry out reforming directly at the anode of the cell, which is already supplied with a nickel-based catalyst. When operated in this way, heat generated during the anode reaction will drive the reformation to convert the hydrocarbon fuel into hydrogen. More usually, however, reforming is be carried out indirectly using a separate catalytic chamber adjacent to the anode. As with direct reforming, the heat for the reaction is supplied from the anode itself. In both cases any carbon monoxide formed will be converted at the anode, as described earlier in this chapter.

Internal reforming allows for the most efficient operation by closely integrating the reformer with the MCFC, so that heat from the cell is used efficiently in the reforming process. However, the internal reformer is complex to engineer and is best suited to smaller MCFC systems. For larger cells an external reformer may be more economical.

The high temperature of the cell when operating, and the consequent insensitivity to impurities in the fuel supplied to the anode means that a MCFC can operate with a variety of fuels in addition to natural gas. One alternative that has been tested extensively is biogas generated from the anaerobic digestion of organic material. Gas generated from coal could also be used a fuel, though some cleanup to remove nitrogen and sulfur compounds would be necessary.

6.5 ACTIVE CARBON DIOXIDE CAPTURE

Since the MCFC consumes carbon dioxide at its cathode and produces it at its anode, the fuel cell offers the possibility of an active means of capturing and sequestering carbon dioxide. In this way the cell acts as a carbon dioxide filter. In a standard commercial cell carbon dioxide that is released into the air stream at the anode must be returned to the cathode in order to support the cell reaction and maintain a steady level of electrolyte. However in a cell designed for carbon capture, the oxygen supply to the anode would be taken from the exhaust of a fossil fuel power plant, flue gases that are heavily laden with carbon dioxide.

When the flue gases pass over the cathode, carbon dioxide and oxygen react, forming carbonate ions that go into solution in the electrolyte. Meanwhile, at the anode, carbon dioxide is produced during the cell electrode reaction involving hydrogen. This results in a relatively concentrated stream of carbon dioxide rich exhaust gas from which it is easier to extract the carbon dioxide that would be the case from the flue gases directly from the fossil fuel power plant. Around 70% or more of the carbon dioxide in the flue gases could be captured in this way.

This arrangement would constitute a form of postcombustion carbon dioxide capture for the fossil fuel power plant. However, it may also be possible to integrate the fuel cell with a gas turbine power plant and a reformer to provide a type of precombustion carbon dioxide capture too. The US company FuelCell Energy is developing the active carbon capture concept with support from the US DOE. In Italy, Ansaldo has also been exploring these configurations.

6.6 COMMERCIAL MCFCs

The most significant route to commercialization of MCFCs has been through a development program supported by the US DOE, in collaboration with FuelCell Energy. This research started in 1976 when the latter company was formed under the name Energy Research Corp for the purpose of developing MCFC technology. In 1993 it began testing a MCFC stack with an internal reformer. This formed the basis for a 2 MW demonstration project in Santa Clara which operated between 1999 and 2000. In 2000 the US DOE injected a further $40m in order to provide the company with the ability to develop a fuel cell production capacity of 50 MW/year by 2002.

By the end of 2007[2] FuelCell Energy had installed 40 MCFC plants in the United States, 15 in Asia, and a small number in Europe. In the middle of the second decade of the 21st century the company had three products with generating capacities of 300 kW, 1.4 MW, and 2.8 MW. Electrical efficiency is 47%.

In Europe FuelCell Energy formed an agreement with DaimlerChrysler subsidiary MTU Friedrichshafen GmbH (MTU) to sell MCFCs which were packaged by the subsidiary MTU CFC solutions and sold as HotModules. The fuel cell activities of MTU were acquired in 2012 by Fuel Cell Energy Solutions, a joint venture between FuelCell Energy and Fraunhofer IKTS. This is now the main source of MCFC fuels cells in Europe.

The other main center of MCFC technology is South Korea. Posco Energy has been developing MCFC technology since 2000 in collaboration with the national utility KEPCO and operated a prototype 125 kW system with an external reformer in 2010. Meanwhile in 2007, Posco

[2]*International Status of MCFC Technology*, Angelo Moreno and Stephen McPhail (ENEA—Hydrogen and Fuel Cell Project, Rome, Italy) and Roberto Bove (Joint Research Centre—Institute for Energy, Petten, The Netherlands), 2008.

Energy also became a partner of FuelCell Energy with manufacturing and distribution agreement.

A French company, Franco Cell, is also developing a MCFC system, based on the use of the ethanol reformation to provide a methane stream suitable to fuel a standard MCFC stack. The company hopes to provide small power plants for French Caribbean islands. Plants will use an external ethanol reformer and have a generating capacity of 3.3 MW. They are likely to use standard MCFC stacks.

6.7 APPLICATIONS

The MCFC is a complex fuel cell and is only economical to manufacture in sizes of around 100 kW or larger. This means that the fuel cells are not suitable for small domestic commercial installations. However, institutions such as hospitals, schools, and some larger commercial operations that can use both electricity and high-grade heat are potential customers. In South Korea several large MCFC power plants have been built, including a 59 MW facility that provides both power and district heating to the city of Hwaseong. Meanwhile in Europe, MCFC units are being developed for marine use. However, the technology remains relatively expensive and cost reductions will be necessary to appeal to more than niche or government supported markets.

CHAPTER 7

The Solid Oxide Fuel Cell

The solid oxide fuel cell (SOFC) is a high-temperature fuel cell with an operating temperature of between 600°C and 1000°C. It is unique among fuel cells in that its electrolyte is a ceramic solid oxide that can conduct oxygen ions, making it the complement of the more traditional low-temperature cells where the electrolyte conducts hydrogen ions. The solid structure of the electrolyte means that high temperatures are necessary in order to achieve sufficient solid-state ionic conductivity. However, the cells are potentially the simplest and most rugged of all fuel cells and offer very long lifetimes.

Exploration of solid electrolyte fuel cells started in the 1930s in Europe and was continued in the 1940s in Russia, without significant progress. Attention switched to high-temperature liquid electrolytes in the 1950s (see Chapter 6) although interest in solids persisted. However, it was not until the 1970s and 1980s that significant success was achieved.

Since then the potential of a robust and simple solid-state fuel cell system has led to a large number of SOFC programs and products aimed at a range of different applications. These include small, portable fuel cells offering ten to hundreds of watts, domestic combined heat and power systems based on kilowatt scale fuel cells, much larger systems for both mobile and stationary applications. Very large utility scale power plants are also under development.

Although there are now a wide range of SOFCs available, the technology has proved one of the most difficult to master. Costs are still relatively high but they are falling, particularly in areas where government funding is supporting development and installation.

Fuel Cells. DOI: http://dx.doi.org/10.1016/B978-0-08-101039-6.00007-8

7.1 THE HISTORY OF THE SOFC

Interest in solid electrolyte fuel cells can be traced back until the 1930s but from then until the 1970s it proved extremely difficult to find solid materials that could offer significant oxygen ion conductivity while not reacting at the high operating temperatures with the fuel or air streams required to drive the fuel cell. However, the attraction of a solid, high-temperature cell with high efficiency and tolerance to carbon monoxide continued to prove tantalizing.

During the 1970s the US Department of Energy provided support to the US company Westinghouse for the development of an SOFC. This, the most high-profile early work on practical SOFC stacks, eventually led to a unique tubular SOFC stack structure and proved the viability of the solid electrolyte fuel cell.

Even so the development of the technology remained difficult. Pilot scale stacks were tested but no commercial SOFC was launched although a 100 kW stack was tested in 1997. A hybrid fuel cell/turbine system aimed at the utility market was also tested. Meanwhile in 1998 the fossil fuel business of Westinghouse was taken over by German company Siemens and work on the fuel cell technology passed to Siemens Westinghouse. Development initially continued with the aim of launching a commercial product, but this faltered in 2008 and appears to have been abandoned.

While the tubular technology developed by Westinghouse and Siemens Westinghouse was the highest profile early SOFC work, the tubular cell design was expensive to manufacture. From the early days of SOFC research, there had always been interest in simple planar cells too, and in the last two to three decades, these have become the focus for much more intense development. Planar cells now form the basis for many of the SOFC stacks that are available in different markets across the world although tubular cells are still under development too.

7.2 THE SOFC PRINCIPLE

The primary component of the SOFC is a solid ceramic electrolyte. This solid metal oxide is an insulator that will not conduct electricity. However, it is capable of conducting oxygen ions and this makes it suitable for a fuel cell electrolyte.

Being a solid, the ceramic has significant advantages over all other types of fuel cell. The electrolyte itself is expected to remain stable for very long periods, making the lifetime of a solid oxide cell the longest of any current design. There are no liquids to seal, eliminating a major engineering problem as well as removing a source of electrode erosion common in other cell types. In addition, a fully solid-state device makes fabrication simpler, in principle at least, as the electrodes can be applied directly to the ceramic electrolyte surface using simple solid-state deposition techniques.

While the SOFC offers all these advantages, it has one major disadvantage. It is extremely difficult to gain sufficient oxygen ion conductivity through the ceramic electrolyte to make a fuel cell practical. In order to achieve, this requires extremely high temperatures and most research has focussed on operating temperatures in the region of 800–1000°C. Lower temperature operation is feasible and some materials show good conductivity down to 600–650°C but for the main ceramic metal oxide used to make SOFCs the conductivity below 800°C is too low for practical cells. Other materials are being explored with the aim of achieving adequate conductivity at 600°C or lower but none has proved economically viable so far. In addition, the high operating temperature allows internal reformation of hydrocarbon fuels but 600°C is considered the lower limit before it becomes necessary to consider an external reformer.

The high temperature is necessary to provide sufficient thermal energy to the solid crystal structure for oxygen ions to be able to migrate though the ceramic. Even so, there is little conductivity in the pure metal oxide electrolyte. In order to enhance it the ceramic material is doped with a small amount of a different metal oxide material that disrupts the orderly structure, introducing vacancies or holes in the crystal framework that allow oxygen ions to hop from site to site. This strategy is effective and at 1000°C the conductivity of the doped oxide can be as high as for a liquid electrolyte.

The cell reaction, as with most fuel cells, is that between hydrogen and oxygen to produce water. However in the SOFC, this reaction is mediated by oxygen ions. These oxygen ions are generated at the cathode which is supplied with molecular oxygen from air.

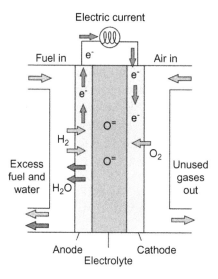

Figure 7.1 The solid oxide fuel cell. Source: Wikipedia commons.

During cell operation, oxygen molecules from air are adsorbed onto the surface of the cathode and dissociate at the high temperature to form oxygen atoms. These atoms each take two electrons from the external electrical circuit that connects cathode and anode, forming oxygen ions (see Fig. 7.1). The oxygen ions can then enter the ceramic electrolyte structure and migrate through it to the anode, driven by a concentration and voltage gradient.

Meanwhile, hydrogen is supplied to the anode of the cell where hydrogen molecules are adsorbed and dissociate into hydrogen atoms. These hydrogen atoms then give up an electron each to the external circuit, forming hydrogen ions which can react with the oxygen ions that migrate through the electrolyte toward to anode to form molecules of water. The water is produced as water vapor which can be carried away in an excess supply of gas to the anode. However, it may also take part in an internal fuel reformation reaction at the electrode.

The cell reactions are shown below.

$$\text{Cathode reaction: } O_2 + 4e^- = 2O^{2-}$$

$$\text{Anode reaction: } 2H_2 = 4H^+ + 4e^-$$

$$\text{Overall reaction: } 2H_2 + 2O_2 = 2H_2O$$

The most common material for the ceramic oxide electrolyte is zirconium oxide (ZrO_2—zirconia). This has a low conductivity for oxygen ions, even at 1000°C. However, if it is doped with another oxide of slightly different structure—usually yttrium oxide (Y_2O_3)—vacancies are introduced into the crystal structure and these increase the oxygen ion conductivity significantly. Zirconia is readily available, cheap and easy to process, making it economically the most attractive material SOFC electrolyte material available today, even though there are other materials with better oxygen ion conductivity at lower temperatures.

In order to reduce its resistance, the electrolyte layer will be extremely thin, typically $10-100\,\mu$m. Electrodes are then attached to the ceramic electrolyte layer to complete the cell. The high temperatures lead to relatively large thermal expansion when a cell is heated from ambient to its operating temperature. To avoid the ceramic electrolyte cracking and separating from the electrode layers, these must be designed to have similar thermal coefficients of expansion. Even so, heating a cell from cold to its operating temperature must be carried out cautiously to prevent thermal gradients forming which could exacerbate the problem.

The cathode of the cell is continuously exposed to oxygen at high temperature and it must be resistant to chemical oxidation by the gas. The most stable cathode materials are noble metals, silver, and gold, but these are expensive so a ceramic oxide is more usually used. The most common in use is lanthanum magnatite ($LaMnO_3$) doped with strontium to enhance its electrical conductivity.

The anode, meanwhile, is exposed to hydrogen during cell operation and must resist chemical reduction by the gas. Metals are the best anode materials and for the SOFC nickel is most commonly used, usually dispersed in a metal ceramic composite (called a cermet) that has a thermal coefficient matched to that of the electrolyte.

One of the additional advantages of the SOFC is that it is capable of using a range of fuels directly. At the high cell operating temperature methane from natural gas can be reformed directly at the anode according to the reaction:

$$CH_4 + H_2O = CO + 3H_2$$

Since water is generated at the anode during cell operation, this reaction can be carried out without additional water. Moreover, the carbon monoxide that is produced in this reaction can also act as a fuel for the cell, reacting with migrating oxygen ions to form carbon dioxide:

$$2CO + 2O^- = 2CO_2 + 4e^-$$

Alternatively, carbon monoxide may undergo a water shift reaction with the water molecules at the anode to produce more hydrogen.

The cell voltage from a single SOFC is around 0.7–0.8 V. In order to increase this to create a more useful device, cells are arranged in series, back to back with the anode of one cell connected directly to the cathode of the next to create a cell stack. The interconnecting structures are designed so that the fuel and air can be directed to the two electrodes without mixing. As with the other components of an SOFC, these interconnecting structures must be made of materials with thermal coefficients of expansion that match those of the cell. Either metals or ceramics can be employed but it is normally easier to match thermal properties by using ceramics. The current that a single cell can provide depends upon the surface area. Single cells can have large surface areas but stacks may also be connected in parallel to create the required power output. Practical SOFC efficiency is generally around 50% although pilot scale plants have achieved up to 57% in small fuel cell stacks.

There are a number of reactions that can poison or damage the solid oxide. The material is particularly susceptible to sulfur poisoning and this must be removed from any fuel gas. However, provided care is taken cells are capable of extremely long lifetimes. Pilot scale stacks have operated for in excess of 60,000 h and an operational life of 20 years or more for a stack should be achievable.

7.3 ELECTROLYTES AND CELL STRUCTURES

There are two primary designs for the SOFC, the planar cell and the tubular cell. Each has its advantages. The planar cell, in which the electrolyte and the electrodes are formed into a flat wafer, is the easiest, and therefore the cheapest to fabricate. However, the interconnecting structures that are required to form cells into stacks have to feed air to the cathode of one cell and hydrogen or fuel to the anode of the adjacent cell without allowing the two to mix. Sealing

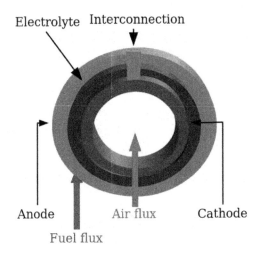

Electrolyte Interconnection

Anode   Air flux   Cathode

Fuel flux

Figure 7.2 Cross-section of a tubular SOFC. Source: Wikipedia commons.

high-temperature solid-state cells to prevent the gas feeds mixing is one of the main challenges for planar cells. Gas management to ensure even supply across the planar surface is also an important consideration.

Tubular cells avoid this sealing and gas supply management problem. The tubular cell is formed from a ceramic electrolyte tube, sealed at one end. One of the electrodes is applied to the inside of this tube and the second to the outside, as shown in Fig. 7.2. In operation, air is introduced into the inside of the tube while the fuel or hydrogen is fed to the outside, with the tube itself preventing any mixing. The tubular cell structure itself is more difficult to fabricate than the simple planar structure.

The electrolyte and electrodes of a SOFC are designed to be extremely thin in order to achieve good conductivity in each component. However, this also renders them structurally weak. To overcome this, one of the layers is normally make much thicker than is necessary in order to provide the necessary structural integrity. Some cells are "electrolyte supported." This requires a thicker electrolyte layer of up to 200 μm or more which reduces the conductivity, so a higher operational temperature is required to compensate. More common, particularly in planar cells is an "anode supported" structure in which the nickel cermet is the thickest component. The other common alternative is that the cell is built onto a metal support that acts as a current collector and as an interconnector between stacked cells.

The most common material for the electrolyte in SOFCs is zirconium oxide doped with yttrium oxide. This material starts to show oxide ion conductivity above 800°C and can be operated between 800°C and 1100°C. The material shows high stability in both the oxidizing and the reducing environment found at either electrode and it is possible to make the electrolyte layer extremely thin to reduce internal resistance. Other materials have been tested including bismuth oxide, cerium oxide, and tantalum oxide. Doped cerium can provide good oxygen ion conductivity at a lower temperature than zirconia but suffers from higher electronic conductivity which creates a short-circuit loss through the cell.

Another group of crystalline materials called perovskites have also shown promising properties. One, doped $LaGaO_3$, has shown good low-temperature conductivity but has stability problems.

The anode of cells based on zirconia use a nickel/zirconia ceramic. This is porous, providing a large surface area for the gas/solid phase reactions that must take place, while the zirconia matrix has a similar thermal expansion to the electrolyte since they are based on the same material. The oxygen reaction at the cathode is generally the slowest in the cell and therefore the performance limiting process. In the SOFC the cathode is generally a perovskite such as doped $LaMnO_3$, as noted above, or $LaSrO_3$. As with the anode, the cathode must be porous, it must provide a high surface area to allow fast oxygen reaction and its thermal expansion coefficient must match that of the electrolyte.

7.4 SOFC-TURBINE HYBRIDS

The theoretical efficiency of an SOFC fuel cell is around 60% and practical cells can achieve more than 50% fuel to electricity conversion efficiency. The high operating temperature means that the exhaust gases from the cell contain a large amount of heat energy and this energy can be captured and used in industrial process heating or to raise steam for a steam turbine to generate more electricity. A hybrid plant combining an SOFC with a waste heat boiler and small steam turbine might be expected to increase overall conversion efficiency to 60% while still leaving some exhaust heat which might be used produce hot water or heat for space heating.

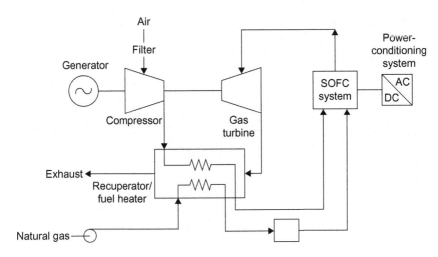

Figure 7.3 Block diagram of a hybrid SOFC-gas turbine fuel cell power plant.

A more complex but potentially more efficient configuration involves integrating the SOFC with a small gas turbine, as shown in Fig. 7.3. This requires the fuel cell to be operated under pressure. A gas turbine consists of two sections, a compressor and a turbine. In the SOFC-gas turbine hybrid plant, air is drawn into the compressor of the gas turbine and compressed and then this pressurized air is used to supply the cathode of the fuel cell with oxygen. After passing through the fuel cell the air becomes heated and the hot, pressurized exhaust gas is then passed into the turbine stage of the microturbine where it provides enough energy to drive the unit's compressor and a small generator. A pilot scale project of this type in the United States in the first decade of the 21st century achieved around 53% efficiency. For a large, utility scale, system of this type efficiency could potentially rise close to 70%.

In a very large utility system it might be feasible to take this a stage further. The exhaust from the gas turbine will still contain high-grade heat and this could be used to raise steam for a steam turbine, in effect integrating a combined cycle plant and an SOFC. Efficiency in this configuration might rise to 75% but it would only be economically feasible at a very large scale.

7.5 FUEL PROCESSING

A power plant based on the SOFC can exploit a variety of fuels including pure hydrogen, natural gas, and a range of other hydrocarbon fuels. Fuels other than hydrogen need to be reformed first if they are to be used in the fuel cell. It is possible to carry out reforming directly at the anode of the fuel cell but complete reforming at this stage introduces a range of potential poisoning problems so it is often more practical to reform the fuel at an earlier stage. This can either be in an external reformer or, more usually in a high-temperature fuel cell, in an internal reformer adjacent to the anode that takes advantage of the heat energy available. Internal reforming is most practical in larger SOFC systems. For smaller systems an external reformer is more practical.

Depending on the fuel, the reformer will also include a system to remove any sulfur compounds because sulfur ions can migrate into the electrolyte in place of oxygen, poisoning it. It is important to ensure that complete reformation of the hydrocarbon fuels takes place, leaving only carbon monoxide or hydrogen, because if hydrocarbons reach the electrode they may be converted to carbon which can be deposited onto the surface (a process known as coking), reducing its activity. New electrode materials are being developed that offer better reformation reactivity and resistance to coking of the electrode surface. These may allow SOFCs to directly process fuels such as biogas.

Reforming of natural gas and other hydrocarbon fuels normally leaves a mixture of carbon monoxide and hydrogen. For low-temperature cells, carbon monoxide is a catalyst poison so a second, water shift reaction is carried out to convert the carbon monoxide into carbon dioxide and more hydrogen (see Chapter 4). Since the SOFC can use carbon monoxide as fuel in addition to hydrogen, there is no need to carry the water shift reaction. This simplifies the design.

7.6 COMMERCIAL SOFC CELLS AND APPLICATIONS

SOFCs are capable of supplying power in a wide variety of situations, from small portable power for electronic devices to utility scale power plants. Much of the development work aimed at large scale systems has been based on the tubular cell design. From the 1970s until around 2008, one of the main projects was being developed by Westinghouse, and later Siemens Westinghouse. That project appears to have lapsed but similar technology is still being developed in Japan. Meanwhile the

UK company Rolls Royce also launched a major SOFC development program based on tubular cell design with the aim of developing utility scale hybrid power plants that combine SOFC and gas turbines technology. The Korean company LG took a controlling stake in the Rolls Royce fuel cell company in 2012 but is continuing with hybrid plant development.

Another type of tubular technology is the microtubular SOFC. The more established tubular designs have tubes with diameters or around 15 mm. However, these have a relatively high thermal mass and heating them to operating temperature takes a long time. An alternative is to build much narrower tubes, with diameters that range from a few millimeters to the submillimeter level. Such cells can be built with very thin electrolyte layers, reducing the internal cell resistance, and the low thermal mass provides a relatively low resistance to rapid changes in the temperature, making this type of cell attractive for small-scale applications.

The alternative, planar cell design is much easier to fabricate than the tubular cell. However, the gas management for these cells is more complex. Nevertheless there are a range of commercial cells available based on the planar technology. These include units that can supply hundreds of kilowatts of power for commercial applications and much smaller domestic combined heat and power units that use a SOFC stack to provide home power and then capture the waste heat for heating and hot water. This type of technology is being promoted in Japan and there are a number of European designs too. At the lower end of the generating capacity scale, there are also small portable units based on planar SOFC technology.

CHAPTER 8

Direct Methanol Fuel Cell

The direct methanol fuel cell (DMFC) is a polymer membrane fuel cell, similar in concept to the proton exchange membrane fuel cell discussed in Chapter 4. The major difference is that in the DMFC the fuel supplied to the anode of the cell is not gaseous hydrogen but methanol in the liquid form. The methanol can react directly at the cell electrode without the need for external reforming. This simplifies the cell, reducing costs. The use of a liquid rather than a gaseous fuel is extremely attractive as it makes fuel handling much easier. The main application for the DMFC today is as a portable power supply with fuel provided in cartridges but it is of interest to the automotive industry too where the use of a high energy density, liquid fuel in a fuel cell—powered engine has many attractions as a replacement for gasoline.

Initial research into the DMFC was carried out in the 1950s and 1960s, then revived during the 1990s. This early research focussed on liquid electrolytes. Attention switched to polymer electrolytes in the 1990s following the success of the proton exchange membrane fuel cell. The first DMFCs of this type exhibited low current densities but this has subsequently been improved. However, efficiency remains poor, with practical cell efficiencies around 25%, low compared to other types of fuel cell. The interest in liquid fuel—based fuel cells has also extended to ethanol and the equivalent direct ethanol fuel cell (DEFC) is also under development. Ethanol is a bio-fuel and so potentially offers an attractive zero-emissions fuel cell strategy.

8.1 THE HISTORY OF THE DMFC

The electrochemical oxidation of methanol was first studied by E Muller in 1922, but it was not until the early 1950s that its use in a fuel cell was considered. Initial research concentrated on alkaline electrolytes because the methanol reaction at the anode of a cell is fast in

Fuel Cells. DOI: http://dx.doi.org/10.1016/B978-0-08-101039-6.00008-X

an alkaline medium. In addition, there was already experience with the alkaline fuel cells (Chapter 3) to draw on as these were being developed for space applications.

Much of this early work focussed on trying to identify suitable electrode materials and catalysts to enhance the speed of the electrode reactions. One of the early designs that produced significant power was developed by scientists at US company Allis Chalmers and demonstrated in 1963. The 750 W stack used a potassium hydroxide electrolyte, a platinum—palladium anode and a silver cathode.[1] The operating temperature was 50°C.

Although some success was achieved no major progress was made because alkaline electrolytes in a DMFC have one major drawback; the alkali reacts with carbon dioxide produced at the anode, generating carbonates which can poison the electrolyte and the electrode. Although cell regeneration is possible, cell life was severely limited.

The problem with carbonate production stimulated a shift of interest to acidic electrolytes in the 1960s. Early DMFCs using acidic electrolytes were developed by companies including Shell, Exxon, and Hitachi. These typically used sulfuric acid as the electrolyte and platinum as the electrode catalyst. In 1968 scientists at Shell identified platinum—ruthenium as an effective anode catalyst for these cells. This remains the most common anode catalyst in use in the current generation of DMFCs.

There was a major change at the beginning of the 1990s when research switched from liquid electrolytes to solid acidic polymer membrane electrolytes. The led to an stepwise improvement in cell performance. Polymer membrane electrolytes remain the most successful for DMFCs but efficiencies and lifetimes of cells are still low compared to other fuel cell designs. Even so, commercial products based on the DMFC are now available, aimed particularly at markets where the high energy density of the fuel makes them attractive even though overall efficiency is low.

[1]Direct Methanol Fuel Cells: History, Status and Perspectives, Antonino Salvatore Aricò, Vincenzo Baglio, and Vincenzo Antonucci, in Electrocatalysis of Direct Methanol Fuel Cells, edited by Hansan Liu and Jiujun Zhang, Wiley-VCH Verlag GmbH, 2009.

8.2 THE DMFC PRINCIPLE

The DMFC is novel because its cell reaction combines the reformation of methanol to generate hydrogen at the anode of the cell with the reaction of this hydrogen at the same electrode to produce electricity. Oxygen provided from air at the second electrode completes the cell reaction. A schematic of the cell is shown in Fig. 8.1. The simplicity of the process, with no need for an external reformer, makes the DMFC immensely attractive. However, the process is not quite so simple as it seems. The reformation of methanol at the anode requires water, which is consumed during the process. This consumption of water is balanced by water production at the cathode of the cell. In a practical cell a way must be found to maintain water balance, ideally by returning water from the cathode to the anode. Unfortunately, this adds to the complexity of the cell and in many cases the water from the cathode is simply discarded and water is provided to the anode my mixing it with the methanol fuel.

The reaction taking place at the anode of a DMFC with an acidic, proton-conducting electrolyte can be expressed in terms of the two equations below. The first shows methanol and water being reformed at the electrode surface to produce carbon dioxide and hydrogen. The second is the classic fuel cell process in which hydrogen atoms at the anode release an electron each and the migrate into the proton-conducting acidic electrolyte.

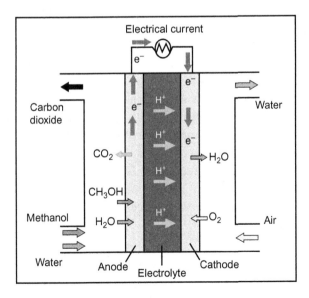

Figure 8.1 The direct methanol fuel cell.

Anode reactions: $CH_3OH + H_2O = CO_2 + 6H$
$$H = H^+ + e^-$$

Oxygen is supplied to the cathode, normally from air, and oxygen molecules are adsorbed onto the electrode surface where they dissociate to form oxygen atoms. These atoms take electrons from the external circuit, forming oxygen ions which then combine with protons migrating through the electrolyte to form water molecules. These two processes are shown below.

Cathode reactions: $O_2 = 2O$
$$2O + 4e^- + 4H^+ = 2H_2O$$

The complete reaction taking place is the sum of these two processes:

$$2CH_3OH + 3O_2 = 2CO_2 + 4H_2O$$

As this equation shows, the process is the electrochemical "combustion" of methanol in air and the simplicity of the process makes it extremely attractive for a variety of applications. The reaction with ethanol in the DEFC is slightly more complex as ethanol contains a two carbon atom–chain structure but follows a similar pattern which is again the electrochemical combustion of the alcohol in air.

The DMFC is a relatively low-temperature cell with a typical operating temperature of $50-130°C$. The electrode reactions in this temperature range are slow and effective catalysts are required to speed them to achieve a reasonable current density. The catalyst used at the anode of a DMFC is platinum mixed with ruthenium. The platinum catalyzes both the reformation reaction and the electrode cell reaction while the ruthenium helps reduce electrode poisoning from carbon monoxide that is generated during the methanol reformation reaction. The catalyst is deposited onto a porous carbon carrier that acts current collector and provides a large surface area for the catalyzed reaction. The cathode is fabricated from a similar porous carbon matrix that has pure platinum deposited onto its surface.

Since the DMFC consumes water at one electrode and produces it at the second, water management is an important aspect of DMFC design. As already noted, the simplest method is to provide water to the anode of the cell by mixing it with the methanol fuel. Meanwhile at the cathode, the water generated during the cell reaction is swept away as water vapor with excess air supplied to that electrode. While this simplifies the design, it is a handicap for portable applications because it means that the methanol fuel must be diluted with water, reducing its energy density. High energy density is one of the key attractions of methanol.

The alternative strategy is to capture the water generated at the cathode and return it to the anode. This can be carried out in a large DMFC with the addition of a condenser and pump. These components and the necessary pipework will add to the complexity of the cell and reduce overall efficiency since energy will be used to pump the water across the cell. Nevertheless, it can be cost effective for large DMFC stacks. Such complex systems appear impractical for small DMFCs aimed at portable applications and developers are exploring passive means of transferring water across the cell. Miniature pumps are also being considered.

Another major limitation of the DMFC is a process called methanol crossover in which methanol from the anode passes through the polymer membrane electrode to the cathode, effectively short-circuiting the cell chemically. Instead of reforming and contributing to the fuel cell reaction, the methanol that crosses to the cathode through the electrolyte simply reacts with oxygen directly at the electrode surface, the reaction catalyzed by the platinum present there.

Methanol crossover was a major problem in liquid electrolytes. The introduction of polymer membranes improved performance in this respect. However, conventional polymer membranes for DMFCs, which are identical to those used in proton exchange membrane fuel cells (PEMFCs) described in Chapter 4 are still permeable to methanol. While a small amount of methanol crossover is not necessarily and major handicap, the bigger issue is that when methanol reacts with oxygen at the cathode it will generate some carbon monoxide and this will poison the platinum catalyst. New membranes may be able to solve the problem if they have lower methanol permeability.

Methanol crossover is one of a number of mechanisms that lead to the degradation of an operating DMFC. The rate of degradation of these cells is much faster than is found in other low-temperature cells and this limits their lifetimes. Cells being developed for commercial applications can achieve lifetimes of over 2000 h. This is probably adequate for small portable applications such as providing power for a laptop computer or phone but is not adequate for most stationary applications.

Another limitation of the DMFC is its efficiency. In theory an efficiency of 40% should be possible but practical efficiencies are generally around 25% or less. Low efficiency might be an acceptable trade-off for high energy density and extreme portability but again it limits the utility of the technology for more conventional stationary applications where energy cost is an important factor. DMFCs also have a lower power density than PEMFCs and tend to require more precious metal catalyst than their competitors, adding to the cell cost.

8.3 MEMBRANES AND CATALYSTS

The standard DMFC utilizes an acidic polymer membrane usually made from perfluorosulfonic acid, an acidic polymer similar in structure to teflon that when hydrated will conduct protons. The most common of these materials, called Nafion, was discovered and patented by DuPont in the late 1960s. While these membranes can be used to build effective cells, they suffer from methanol crossover and cannot operate at temperatures above 100°C without the danger of water loss and dehydration.

A range of alternative electrolytes are being explored. These include some solid polymer electrolytes that offer the potential to reduce methanol crossover significantly. For high-temperature operation, it may be possible to construct composite membranes that contain a traditional polymer mixed with dispersed solid materials such as silicon oxide that help retain water within the membrane or improve overall proton conductivity. This strategy has been used to make a DMFC that could operate at up to 145°C.

An more recent approach is to return to the early days of DMFC research and develop alkaline membranes. The oxygen reaction at the anode of a fuel cell is generally much faster in an alkaline electrolyte than in an acidic electrolyte and since this is generally the limiting process, there are clear advantages to using alkali media. However, a liquid alkali electrolyte will react with carbon dioxide generated at the anode, producing carbonates that will poison the electrolyte. Recently some success has been achieved by using anion ion-exchange membranes in place of the traditional membrane in a DMFC. This type of membrane will conduct hydroxyl (OH^-) ions. These are generated at the cathode of a fuel cell of this type, then transported through the membrane to the anode where they react with hydrogen ions resulting from the methanol reformation reaction to form water. However, these membranes can still suffer from methanol crossover and from carbonate and bicarbonate generation at the anode.

The most common anode catalyst in an acidic membrane DMFC remains ruthenium/platinum even though this was discovered 50 years ago. The two metals are in the form of an alloy with around 50% ruthenium, supported on a carbon electrode structure. Although other metal catalysts have been tested, none has shown the effectiveness of Pt–Ru. A similar electrode structure has been utilized for alkaline membranes, but the faster reaction speeds in the alkaline medium means that cheaper nickel-based catalytic material can also be used. The cathode catalyst for both types of cell is generally platinum.

8.4 APPLICATIONS

The most promising application of DMFCs is to supply power to microelectronic devices such as mobile phones, tablets, and laptop computers. The energy density of a DMFC, at around 6000 Wh/kg is around 10 times that of a typical lithium ion battery[1] so a similar sized fuel cell power supply should last 10 times longer. Alternatively much smaller and lighter power supplies could be built to provide a similar capacity to a battery. Recharging is avoided too because the fuel comes in a small canister which, once exhausted, can be immediately replaced with a new one.

The power output of these small DMFCs varies with the application. For example, a typical mobile phone requires around up to 2 W of power when operating and less than one-tenth of that during standby. The fuel cell could also be used for larger mobile communications applications, an area that has attracted military interest. Stacks for this type of application would need to be larger than for phones, in the range of 10–100 W. Mobile computers also require large power supplies than phones.

The other potential area of application is for automotive power. A fuel cell that runs on a liquid fuel would be much easier to integrate into existing vehicle fuel supply systems based on gasoline than one that requires gaseous fuel while the high energy density of the fuel means that much greater ranges are possible. However, the fuel cell is in competition with batteries in electric vehicles and where fuel cell vehicles are being developed the primary technology under consideration is the PEMFC. If DMFCs can quickly overcome problems relating to efficiency and power density they may be able to challenge in this market. Otherwise, they may be left behind.

In the meantime there are one or two commercial products aimed at niche markets. The most readily available are small devices with power outputs in the range of 25–50 W that are designed to supply electrical power to caravans, and similar devices aimed at small industrial and commercial applications. The cost of these devices is still too high for the technology to expect to capture a wide market.

CHAPTER 9

Fuel Cells and the Environment

The fuel cell would appear to be the ideal clean energy source for providing electricity in situations where electricity generated from renewable sources such as wind, solar, or hydro power is either not available or not appropriate. Most fuel cells require only two inputs, hydrogen and oxygen, the latter from air, and when operating their only reaction products are water and some heat. They are simple, compact, and easily scalable so that the efficiency of a small fuel cell is nominally the same at that of a large cell. Moreover, the overall efficiency of a fuel cell when fed with pure hydrogen is comparable or better than that of most fossil fuel power plants, while advanced hybrid fuel cell power plants may be the most efficient type of power plant yet devised.

The reality today is somewhat more complex. Hydrogen is not widely available for fuel cell power plants and so most have to generate hydrogen by reforming natural gas or another hydrocarbon fuel. This reduces overall efficiency because energy is required to drive the reforming process. The latter will also generate similar volumes of carbon dioxide as would result from burning the fuel directly in a fossil fuel power plant, although the catalytic reforming process leads to lower emissions of other pollutants such nitrogen oxides. Over the long term, perhaps looking at a 50-year horizon, hydrogen may become a readily available fuel. If that happens then the full benefits of fuel cells will be available. In the meantime they still have many advantages.

Fuel cells offer a relatively clean and environmentally benign option for power generation. Power plants based on fuel cells are relatively compact and the fuel cell stacks themselves have no moving parts although the system may require pumps for cooling and fuel supply. The more complex hybrid systems include turbines too. Simple fuel cells are quiet and their low emissions make them suitable for use in urban areas where other types of power plant are difficult to integrate. The relatively high efficiency of fuel cells is also an advantage.

Fuel Cells. DOI: http://dx.doi.org/10.1016/B978-0-08-101039-6.00009-1

However, the devices are still a niche technology and costs are high. The price will only fall when production volumes increase.

9.1 FUEL CELLS, EMISSIONS, AND EFFICIENCY

In its ideal form the fuel cell exploits the chemical reaction between hydrogen and oxygen to produce water, electrical power, and a certain amount of waste heat. In this ideal form the fuel cells have very little environmental impact. However, the realization of that ideal scenario is marred by the fact that hydrogen is not readily available in most locations. There are a small number of hydrogen refueling stations for fuel cell−powered vehicles but the number is limited and there is no hydrogen supply network similar to the gas supply network. So, for most stationary power applications the gas must be provided in cylinders or it must be manufactured on site. The latter is the favored option.

Most fuel cells for small domestic or commercial applications reform natural gas to provide hydrogen. The reforming is carried out catalytically and conditions are different to those in a combustion plant or engine. This leads to a different emissions profile for the main toxic or hazardous emissions.

The temperature at which the reactions take place, even within high-temperature solid oxide fuel cells designed for domestic heat and power use, is low compared to fossil fuel combustion systems. This results in little or no nitrogen oxides formation. There may be some carbon monoxide but this must be strictly controlled for low-temperature cells, otherwise it will poison the catalyst, while high-temperature cells will consume it as fuel so emissions are usually extremely low. There is also the potential for small amounts of incompletely converted hydrocarbons. Sulfur is a poison in all fuel cells and it must be scrupulously removed from the fuel before use, so sulfur emissions are generally close to zero.

Carbon emissions are a different matter. The reforming of natural gas or any other hydrocarbon fuel produces carbon dioxide as one of the main products. Methanol, the fuel for direct methanol fuel cells, also produces carbon dioxide. The amount of carbon dioxide produced is similar to that produced when the fuel is burned in a gas turbine or piston engine power plant. This means that the relative impact of the

Table 9.1 Efficiencies of Fuel Cells and Typical Fossil Fuel Power Sources	
Type of Power Plant	Efficiency
Alkaline fuel cell	>60%
Proton exchange membrane fuel cell	60% with hydrogen, 40% with reformed natural gas
Phosphoric acid fuel cell	36%–42%
Molten carbonate fuel cell	50%
Solid oxide fuel cell	50%, higher with hybrid system
Direct methanol fuel cell	25%
Gas turbine	46%
Combined cycle power plant	61%
Reciprocating engine	50%

different technologies depends on the overall fuel-to-electrical energy conversion efficiency of each. The more units of electricity that are produced for each unit of natural gas consumed, the lower the emissions per unit of electricity.

The theoretical maximum fuel cell efficiency at ambient temperature is 83% although this falls at higher temperatures. None can reach this level of efficiency but many fuel cells compare favorably with fossil fuel power plants in efficiency terms. Some efficiency figures are shown in Table 9.1.

The phosphoric acid fuel cell has the lowest efficiency, typically 36%–42% when using natural gas, although some manufacturers have claimed slightly higher efficiency. Small phosphoric acid fuel cell systems are used in commercial or public service applications, usually as combined heat and power units. The overall efficiency when heat capture is included is around 87%. This level of efficiency could be matched by a reciprocating engine plant burning natural gas but such a unit would be noisier and produce greater emissions of nitrogen oxides. A diesel engine might have greater electrical efficiency but at the expense of higher emissions, making this type of plant a less suitable alternative.

Proton exchange membrane fuel cells are also available in generating capacities similar to phosphoric acid stacks. They provide a similar efficiency when using reformed natural gas but the amount of heat energy released is lower and they are less suitable for combined heat and power applications. Alkaline fuel cells, also available in this size range, are significantly more efficient than either of these alternatives but they are still too expensive for wide scale use.

For larger stationary applications, either molten carbonate of solid oxide fuel cells are likely to be the most appropriate. Both can achieve close to 50% efficiency with natural gas. The molten carbonate cell generally achieves slightly higher efficiency in a simple fuel cell but the solid oxide fuel cell offers the potential of significantly higher efficiency in a hybrid configuration. The closest direct competitor to these would be an open cycle gas turbine. The best small open derivative gas turbine can reach 46% efficiency when burning natural gas.

For very large stationary applications the most likely fuel cell candidate is a hybrid solid oxide fuel cell plant. Since commercial plants of this type are not yet available, it is difficult to make realistic comparisons but such a configuration should be able to provide power more efficiently that a combined cycle power plant burning natural gas.

There are other advantages that fuel cell power plants offer that are not clear from the overall efficiency figures in Table 9.1. The efficiency of a fuel cell does not depend on the size of the plant. A small plant is as efficient as a large plant using the same technology. In addition, the efficiency does not vary with output, and neither do the emissions levels. In contrast the efficiency of a gas turbine or reciprocating engine power plant will vary with output so that part load efficiency is significantly lower than at full load. Emissions may increase too, particularly if output is varying frequently. These fossil fuel plants offer their best performance when operating at a stable output close to their maximum.

A fuel cell power plant is also fast acting, so that output can change rapidly. This is extremely valuable for load following or grid support facilities. The fuel cell plants may require a significant time to reach their operating temperature but once there they can provide a highly flexible, efficient, and clean power supply. The speed of response of fossil fuel power plants to changes in load varies but most cannot match a fuel cell.

9.2 THE HYDROGEN ECONOMY

To obtain the best from a fuel cell, it must be fueled with hydrogen. This would allow the cell stacks to achieve their highest efficiencies, in some cases higher than those shown in Table 9.1. Performance at this level would be feasible in a hydrogen economy in which hydrogen is used as a replacement for natural gas and is widely available as pipeline fuel.

Of course, this would require the production of massive volumes of hydrogen. Practically, most of this hydrogen would be produced from electricity by the hydrolysis of water. Producing hydrogen from water is a relatively efficient process with current generation electrolyzers capable of 90% efficiency and new systems under development aiming for 94% efficiency. Converting the hydrogen back into electricity using the most efficient fuel cell system, with say an optimistic efficiency of 75% in a hybrid solid oxide fuel cell plant, gives a round trip efficiency of around 71%, or a loss of 31 percentage points.

This is a large energy loss and it must be balanced by some economic gain. The only way this is likely to be economically effective is if the hydrogen is produced from renewable energy power plants such as wind or solar plants that are generating power that would otherwise not to be used. This then becomes a form of energy storage, and as such begins to make good economic sense.

There may be new dangers from switching from fossil fuels to a mixed renewable and hydrogen-based fuel economy. It has been suggested, for example, that a hydrogen fuel manufacturing and supply network will lead to the release of large volumes of hydrogen into the atmosphere which might plausibly have a detrimental effect on the ozone layer, although the science remains to be fully established.

On the other hand replacing fossil fuels with hydrogen enables a relatively simple transition away from the hydrocarbon based fuel economy and presents a feasible long term option that builds on existing infrastructure. This is a long way off today and there is no certainty that it will be realized. Alternatives may be preferred. However, if it was realized, then fuel cells would be expected play a large part in the resulting electricity production system.

9.3 OTHER ENVIRONMENTAL CONSIDERATIONS

There are a range of additional environmental effects associated with fuels cell power plants that are common to most power plants. For a large stationary power plant, there will be disruption associated with the construction phase and with the connection of the plant to a fuel supply and the electricity grid. This will be partly mitigated by the fact that the major components of a fuel cell system are assembled in a factory away from the site and then delivered completed, so the amount and length of the disruption will be minimized. Similar considerations apply when the plant is decommissioned.

All fuel cells release heat as well as producing electricity. In some case this will be captured and used but there will be plants that release this heat into the environment, causing localized thermal changes that may have a discernible impact. There will also be water production which must be managed. The fuel cell reaction will often produce this in the form of water vapor which will have an impact if released straight into the atmosphere. Alternatively, it may be condensed, in which case significant volumes of liquid water will require disposal. However, the latter will be pure water and could be added to the local drinking water supply.

Fuel cells are high technology devices and some of the materials from which they are made are exotic, though they are not generally toxic. The most important of these from an environmental perspective may be platinum which is used as a catalyst in many low-temperature fuel cells. Global platinum reserves are limited and it is one of the most expensive metals available. Reserves were estimated to be 66,000 tonnes at the end of 2015.[1] Low-temperature cells with platinum catalysts are likely to be popular for automotive power units and for small domestic stationary applications. However for many stationary applications, high-temperature fuel cells may be more suitable and these do not need platinum and use nickel instead. There is no suggestion today that global platinum supplies will be threatened by the growth of fuel cells.

Recycling of fuel cell power supplies for small portable applications will become an issue if these become widely popular. The lifetimes for direct methanol fuel cells, which offer one of the best options for this market, are low and the turnover could be large. However, existing recycling networks for batteries should be able to manage these.

---

[1] https://www.statista.com/statistics/273624/platinum-metal-reserves-by-country/.

CHAPTER 10

The Cost of Electricity From Fuel Cells

The cost of electricity from a power plant of any type depends on a range of factors. First there is the cost of building the power station and buying all the components needed for its construction. In addition, most large power projects today are financed using loans so there will also be a cost associated with paying back the loan, with interest. Then there is the cost of operating and maintaining the plant over its lifetime, including fuel costs. Finally, the overall cost equation should include the cost of decommissioning the power station once it is removed from service.

It would be possible to add up all these cost elements to provide a total cost of building and running the power station over its lifetime, including the cost of decommissioning, and then dividing this total by the total number of units of electricity that the power station produced over its lifetime. The result would be the real lifetime cost of electricity from the plant. Unfortunately, such as calculation could only be completed once the power station was no longer in service. From a practical point of view, this would not be of much use. The point in time at which the cost-of-electricity calculation of this type is most needed is before the power station is built. This is when a decision is made to build a particular type of power plant, based normally on the technology that will offer the least cost electricity over its lifetime.

10.1 LEVELIZED COST OF ENERGY MODEL

In order to get around this problem, economists have devised a model that provides an estimate of the lifetime cost of electricity before the station is built. Of course, since the plant does not yet exist, the model requires that a large number of assumptions be made. In order to make this model as useful as possible, all future costs are also converted to the equivalent cost today by using a parameter known as the

Fuel Cells. DOI: http://dx.doi.org/10.1016/B978-0-08-101039-6.00010-8

discount rate. The discount rate is almost the same as the interest rate and relates to the way in which the value of one unit of currency falls (most usually, but it could rise) in the future. This allows, for example, the cost of replacement of a fuel cell stack 20 years into the future to be converted into an equivalent cost today. The discount rate can also be applied the cost of electricity from the fuel cell in 20 years time.

The economic model is called the levelized cost of electricity (LCOE) model. It contains a lot of assumptions and flaws but it is the most commonly used method available for estimating the cost of electricity from a new power plant.

When considering the economics of new power plants the levelized cost is one factor to consider. Another is the overall capital cost of building the generating facility. This has a significant effect on the cost of electricity but it is also important because it shows the financial investment that will have to be made before the power plant generates any electricity. The comparative size of the investment needed to build different types of power stations may determine the actual type of plant built, even before the cost of electricity is taken into account. This is of importance with fuel cells as their capital cost is probably the highest of all generating technologies. Capital cost is usually expressed in terms of the cost per kilowatt of generating capacity to allow comparisons between technologies to me made.

When comparing different types of power station there are other factors that need to be considered too. The type of fuel, if any, that is uses is one. A coal-fired power station costs much more to build than a gas-fired power station but the fuel it burns is relatively cheap. Natural gas is more expensive than coal and it has historically shown much greater price volatility than coal. This means that while the gas-fired station may require lower initial investment, it might prove more expensive to operate in the future if the gas prices rise dramatically. Fuel cells which rely on natural gas will be subject to the same vulnerability.

Renewable power plants can also be relatively expensive to build. However, they normally have no fuel costs because the energy they exploit is from a river, from the wind or from the sun and there is no economic cost for taking that energy. That means that once the renewable power plant has been paid for, the electricity it produces will have a very low cost. All these factors may need to be balanced when making a decision to build a new power station.

10.2 CAPITAL COST

Fuel cell power plants are among the most expensive power plants to install, with an estimated capital cost higher than virtually any other power generating technology. While commercial systems are available for domestic and for small stationary power applications, the technology is still in an early commercial stage of development and production volumes are low. Economies of scale should lead to a fall in capital costs, provided manufacturing volumes increase. In the meantime a fuel cell plant will not be an obvious choice for new power generating capacity unless it involves a specific application where the advantages of the fuel cell—such as very low emission levels and low impact, while providing a reliable supply—are a major consideration, or unless there is some financial support for the fuel cell technology such as is available in some countries for domestic combined heat and power based on fuel cell systems.

The costs of the different fuel cell technologies vary widely too. According to figures from the International Energy Agency (IEA),[1] early commercial alkaline fuel cells are the cheapest to produce, with a cost of $200–$700/kW. However, these cells only have a lifetime of around 5000–8000 h. Small proton exchange membrane fuel cells with a similar lifetime, aimed at automotive applications, have a comparable cost of around $500/kW. For stationary applications much longer operational lifetimes are necessary and consequently the costs are significantly higher. Proton exchange membrane fuel cells, solid oxide fuel cells, phosphoric acid fuel cells and molten carbonate fuel cells aimed at the stationary power market all cost between $3000/kW and $6000/kW and offer lifetimes of 20,000–90,000 h depending upon the technology. Of these, only phosphoric acid fuel cells are considered a mature technology. All the others are considered by the IEA to be early market technologies.

[1]Technology Roadmap: Hydrogen and Fuel Cells, Technical Annex, International Energy Agency, 2015.

Table 10.1 Overnight Capital Cost of Fuel Cell Power Plants[2]	
Year	Overnight Capital Cost ($/kW)
2000	2163
2001	1767
2002	1810
2003	1850
2004	1872
2005	3679
2006	3787
2007	3913
2008	4653
2009	4640
2010	4744
2011	5846
2012	5918
2013	6045
2014	6099
2015	6042
Source: US Energy Information Administration	

Table 10.1 shows the evolution of estimates by the US Energy Information Administration (US EIA) for the overnight cost[3] of fuel cells between 2000 and 2015 as published in its Annual Energy Outlook. The table shows the year in which the report was published in column one. The figures alongside each year are for a fuel cell power plant commissioned the year before and priced in dollars for that year. For the purposes of the estimate, the US EIA has considered a 10 MW molten carbonate fuel cell power plant with a 3-year lead time from construction to entering service.

Cost estimates have changed dramatically over the period covered by the table. In 2000 the overnight capital cost was estimated to be $2163/kW, falling to $1767/kW in 2001 before rising slowly to reach $1872/kW in 2004. The estimate undertook a stepwise increase to $3679/kW in 2005 and continued to increase monotonically from then until 2014 when the estimated capital cost reached $6099/kW. In 2015

[2]The figures in the table are taken from the US Energy Information Administration Assumptions to the Annual Energy Outlook, 2000–15.
[3]The overnight cost is the cost without any consideration of financing costs.

the estimated capital cost fell slightly, to $6042/kW. This is broadly in line with the cost estimate from the IEA, above, which put the cost for a molten carbonate fuel cell at $4000–$6000/kW. The US EIA estimate makes the fuel cell the most expensive type of power plant to install of all those it considered, with the exception of a solid waste combustion plant.

The size of the fuel cell industry remains relatively small with few manufacturers and prices are unlikely to vary widely from country to country. However, prices can be expected to fall if manufacturing volumes increase.

10.3 THE LEVELIZED COST OF ELECTRICITY FROM A FUEL CELL POWER PLANT

Capital cost will be one of the main factors determining the LCOE from a fuel cell power plant for stationary power applications. The cost of fuel and lifetime maintenance costs, particularly if stacks require replacement, will be the other major factors.

Lazard has estimated the LCOE for a range of power generation technologies in the United States.[4] It found that the cost of electricity for a fuel cell power plant to be in the range of $106–$167/MWh for a fuel cell system with a capital cost broadly in line with those discussed above. The technology was not specified but the unit was assumed to be used for distributed generation. This estimate made electricity from the fuel cell slightly more expensive than from a distributed generation solar cell application ($78–$136/MWh) and slightly cheaper than from a solar thermal power plant. It was also cheaper than the power from a diesel engine, or from a small open cycle gas turbine used for peak power generation.

[4]Lazard's Levelized Cost of Energy Analysis—Version 9.0, Lazard, 2015.

Printed in the United States
By Bookmasters